HOW TO CHANGE
YOUR LIFE WITH THE
AMAZING SECRETS
OF HYPNOSIS

*Powerful techniques for achieving
health, happiness and success*

How To
CHANGE YOUR LIFE

WITH THE AMAZING SECRETS OF HYPNOSIS

Powerful Techniques for Achieving:

HEALTH HAPPINESS & SUCCESS

Marcus D'Silva

How to change your life-with the amazing secrets of hypnosis

ISBN-13 978-0-9554446-1-6

Published in the UK in 2009 by New London Publishing Ltd

British library cataloguing in publication data a catalogue record for this book is available from the British library.

Printed by CPI Antony Rowe, Chippenham, Wiltshire

CONTENTS

I dedicate this book to my father, who is the most positive man I know.

INTRODUCTION

It seems like a very long time ago that I walked out of that building on a chilly November evening. I knew I would not be returning, and yet I felt a sense of relief. *It was over at last*, I thought to myself. As I wandered down the street in something resembling a trance, the reality started to hit me. I was officially broke, with nothing but the clothes on my back and a rusty BMW to show for my years of hard work. It was 1993, and that year marked the beginning of a new chapter of my life. For many people, my situation could have been viewed as the end. I was a bankrupt. My business had failed.

All of those years of hard work, and all for nothing, people would say. And yet, I didn't feel quite the same way. Although I felt some disappointment, I also felt that there was a lot I could learn from the experience. There was a part of me, deep, deep down, that knew I had the resources to pick myself up, dust myself off, and start again. I very quickly realised that a proportion of my business failure was to do with the fact that I lacked the skills that are necessary to really excel in business and in life.

The outcome of my experience was a journey of self-discovery. I read hundreds of books, invested in self-improvement courses, and actively sought ways to change my life – to become a person who would succeed rather than fail. I became a therapist and travelled the world, and met interesting, enlightening and inspiring people. Today, I run a hugely successful hypnotherapy practice, and have learned a lot about myself, and others – in particular, how people get into difficulties, and, most importantly, how they find solutions to them.

This is not a book about how to get rich or get ahead in business. It's about how to deal with life's problems and challenges. It's about change. It's about using the power of your own mind to attract the results you want to achieve in your life.

Everything that happens to you – good or bad – provides an opportunity for learning. Some of you may have had a brush with death, or overcome a serious illness. You may have managed to lose 40 pounds of excess weight, or quit smoking after 25 years. You may have lost a business or your job; you may have lost or found the love of your life. All of these things are a catalyst for change, a wonderful opportunity to make further changes to get your life going in the direction you've always wanted, and to achieve your dreams.

If you are reading this book you want to change something in your life. Maybe you haven't yet experienced an event or an achievement that has got you thinking that change is not only necessary but also possible; maybe you feel stuck in a rut and need a road out. Maybe you simply feel that it is time to learn from the things that have gone wrong in your life, and find a practical and achievable way to turn them in a new direction.

So whether you want to develop more self-confidence,

lose weight, stop smoking, reduce stress in your life, form a relationship and make it a success, or simply get yourself moving positively towards your dreams, this book can help you. Do you want to improve your health? Use your mind to achieve more success? Read on …

YES, YOU CAN CHANGE YOUR LIFE!

It has been said that you can have anything you want in life, but that you can't have *everything*. These pearls of wisdom are priceless. Why? Because, let's face it, we want it all! We all want that perfect job, a perfect partner, success, health and wellbeing. But what most of us do not understand is that the one thing holding us back is our own minds. Because we are not aware of how our minds work, and the power they hold, we limit ourselves to a life of mediocrity. We compromise on the things that matter to us – our health, our relationships, and, as a result, our wellbeing and happiness.

The most common goal I hear from my clients is, 'I just want to be happy'. And yet the concept of happiness remains rather elusive. Happiness isn't winning the lottery or emigrating to the other side of the world. It isn't finding the perfect job, or even the perfect person. Why not? Because these represent external, rather than internal, change. Yes, of course, all can create happiness within our lives for short periods of time, but these changes will always be temporary. You can be rich and unhappy, and you can also carry unhappiness to faraway lands and into new relationships and jobs. Real, lasting change begins within and continues its journey there. We have to go inside ourselves to find it.

When we learn to use our minds in a solution-focused way, we can create miracles. The big and little changes that we want in our lives become party to, and the product of, the happiness we create internally. We are able to achieve miracles because we have the tools with which to do that. I see and hear about miracles every day in my practice – people who have suddenly lost 60 pounds of excess weight and made the front page of a popular magazine; people who have suddenly quit smoking after years of addiction, or beaten cancer with a special diet. Miracles happen all the time.

Real change begins within. All of us have made changes in our lives to some degree in the past – that's why we are where we are now. We changed our thought processes, made decisions, or visualised ourselves being different; we actively removed the things we didn't want in our lives.

When we learn to use our minds productively, in a solution-focused way, we are truly able to create miracles. So, are you going to take the plunge and quit that job you hate? Are you are going to finally run that marathon you keep talking about? What about overcoming that phobia that's stopping you from living your life to the full? Is it time to do something about the lack of confidence that is holding you back in your career? No more excuses – now is the time to get your mind working for you.

Change can be simpler than you think. It's about taking some time to relax each day, allowing your mind to loosen up, and putting on hold all those negative beliefs as you focus on what you truly desire. Once you learn how to do this you have the power to re-programme your mind for all the health, happiness and success you want.

THE SECRET OF CHANGE

Change is achievable through one of the oldest secrets on the planet. It's something we use every day of our lives, and it is also a natural phenomenon that can be adopted to enhance our lives in many, many ways. This phenomenon can be traced back millions of years – to Ancient Egypt, Greece, and India. It's been used by countless men and women to create riches and wealth. Millions of people have been healed through its power, and the world of advertising uses it to this day.

What are we talking about? Hypnosis, of course.

When hypnosis is mentioned, most of us envision swinging watches and spaced-out people in a trance. But that's not what we are talking about. Hypnosis is, in actuality, an umbrella term for anything subjective. Hypnosis is a process in which the critical thinking faculties of the mind are bypassed and a type of selective thinking and perception is established. It could, for example, be said that someone meditating or even staring out the window is in a state of hypnosis. In fact, all of us have been in a hypnotic or trance state many times in our life. Each of us experiences this state of mind several times throughout the day.

If you take a walk through the self-help section of a bookshop you will find many books teaching you how to improve your life through meditation, visualisation, positive affirmation and all sorts of mind-control techniques. The truth is that these are all forms of self-hypnosis. Any technique that that takes you inward can be termed hypnotic. Most mind-power systems use hypnotic techniques as their structure. Hypnosis is a life tool, and it is available to everyone who wants to take control of their lives.

HOW TO USE THIS BOOK

The first section of this book explores the nature of how our mind works, and the role that language plays in the process of change. The second section offers ways to overcome specific problems: giving up smoking, losing weight, controlling pain, overcoming fear, and more. By the time you reach the second section, you'll have a good understanding of how change happens. You can then apply these general principles of hypnosis to your daily life, to achieve your life goals.

There are three main ways to employ self-hypnosis:

1. Sitting down for 20 minutes, once or twice every day, and working on your desired change by using the language patterns, imagery techniques and meditations found in this book.

2. Becoming mindful of your 'self-talk', and actively changing it to positive self-talk, using the principles of hypnotic language you are about to discover.

3. A combination of both.

It is also important to understand that hypnosis is taking place all the time, not just when we sit and relax. For example, our negative or positive 'self-talk', the mental chatter that goes on in our minds constantly, has a hypnotising effect in that it creates and then reinforces messages that our brain and, in particular, our subconscious, takes on board.

Ideally, we need to become aware of the thoughts and images that we create in our minds, and to listen to the chatter going on, in order to make changes – changing both the message and the visuals. This takes some practice and patience, but making the commitment to become more aware will open your mind to the most amazing changes. The art of self-hypnosis is rather like learning a new way of communicating with ourselves.

PART I

GET INSIDE YOUR MIND: SELF-HYPNOSIS BASICS

CHAPTER 1

LIFE HYPNOSIS

When you're through changing, you're through.
BRUCE BARTON

Have you ever had the experience of arriving at a familiar destination with no memory of how you got there? You had literally no awareness of the travelling experience. The reason for this apparent amnesia is, in fact, that you were on auto-pilot. You were actually in a trance, and your subconscious mind had become programmed to get you to your destination without consciously thinking about it. You may find that you daydream as you drive and end up at a familiar destination rather than the new destination you were seeking, because your subconscious kicked in and drove you to the place you usually want to go.

These types of experiences happen all the time in daily life. For example, when we first meet someone we automatically reach out and shake hands. Why? Because it has become an unconscious action – we have been programmed to act this way; we have created a habit, just like a smoker who automatically brings a cigarette up to his or her mouth.

Any time that we go within ourselves, we are, technically, in a trance state: daydreaming, looking out the window, imagining a holiday we've just booked, or plotting how we will spend our winnings when that lottery ticket comes good.

It is during these periods of the day that we become

highly suggestible to ourselves, and others. We may find ourselves more open to advertising and marketing messages. We may seem more responsive to people around us. We may also find that we are more in tune with our inner selves.

The most powerful part of life hypnosis is the use of language. Words are magic in action. Words can change beliefs, behaviours and habits. Words can heal and destroy. These words can be our own, or they can come from others. By learning to understand the power they have and the laws that guide them, we can create amazing changes within ourselves. Yes, life is all about persuasion, and persuading ourselves is the key. After all, if we don't persuade ourselves, someone else will.

A good proportion of our lives is spent trying to persuade and influence others: trying to get the girl or the guy to walk down the aisle, angling for more pocket money, selling ourselves for a job we want. This book is, however, about *self*-persuasion – persuading yourself to eat less food, stop smoking cigarettes, become more successful in business, get on an airplane, or whatever you want or need to do in your life. Hypnosis is the best and fastest way to achieve self-persuasion.

YOUR SUBCONSCIOUS MIND

It's amazing! We just don't realise the potential we have within. The subconscious mind is a vast storehouse of knowledge; all of our past life learnings are stored there. While we don't always understand why we do the things we do, our subconscious most certainly does. We need to learn to tap into, or unlock, our subconscious to awaken our inner giant, and allow wonderful things to happen. How do we do this? Hypnosis offers the golden key.

When we have access to our subconscious, we will find out things about ourselves that we didn't know we knew. We can re-frame past failures into positive learnings, and we can reprogramme our minds to create healthier new behaviours. Through this we will be able to change our self-image to one that is healthier, more successful, and happy.

The subconscious mind is clever – smarter than our conscious minds. It is wiser, too, and understands more than we realise. In a nutshell, the subconscious mind is *pure awareness*. It collects information and clues constantly, things that fall outside our conscious awareness. It takes responsibility for many of our daily functions, such as walking, breathing, driving, digesting our food, tapping on a keyboard, and so much more. The subconscious is the unconscious, and throughout this book I will use these two words interchangeably.

The childlike subconscious
In many ways, the subconscious mind is childlike. It takes everything literally, and it is non-logical. Just as children are open to suggestion, ideas and learning – soaking up information like sponges – the subconscious is easily swayed, and open to new things. Children make excellent hypnotic subjects, because their capacity for critical thinking is not yet developed, they are more relaxed and creative, have little sense of time, and are more in tune with their subconscious. Over time, in our search for understanding, we lose touch with our subconscious, which is the part of us that facilitates change, growth and adaptation. We need to return to a childlike state of mind, to open ourselves up so

that we can reach our subconscious. The best way to do that is to relax; the more relaxed we are, the better able we are to bypass our logically-thinking conscious mind.

The feeling mind

The subconscious mind is the feeling mind, and it is responsible for our emotions. All of us have experienced sudden anger and rage, or happiness and bliss. These feelings come from our subconscious, which reacts instinctively. By tapping into our subconscious, we can direct these emotions in a positive way, thereby effecting change. Here's a good example of how this works. A man who finds himself single after many years of marriage feels low and unhappy until he meets a woman he'd really like to get to know. As his feelings develop, he is motivated to lose a few pounds and become fitter. His positive state of mind encourages him to make changes. This is the magic of emotion.

We can imagine how we want to be – look, feel, achieve, etc. – in our imaginations, and we can achieve some success. However, if we add some emotion to the exercise success is guaranteed. Emotion is powerful, and it is a catalyst for action. Desire is *focused* emotion, and when we can acquire desire we can literally move mountains. This is one reason why change does not normally occur unless we *want* it to.

THE POWER OF YOUR IMAGINATION

Imagination is the key to creating the life you desire. When you understand the role your imagination plays, you will have the power to design the life you truly want. Let me explain. Everything you have in your life at the present moment is the product of your imagination. You are the scriptwriter, the editor and the director of your life, and every achievement you make is directed by something you envisioned and imagined.

The subconscious mind cannot tell the difference between what we visualise and what we actually act out. This is one reason why top golfers achieve such good results on the course – because they practise their technique, hole by hole, in their imaginations, before they do it for real. All of us run through scenarios before they happen – imagining what might happen on a first date, a job interview, and even a visit with the bank manager. The problem is that we often imagine the worst-case scenario rather than creating a positive image in our minds. So changing the way we use our imaginations is a great starting point to making lasting changes to our lives. We can use our imaginations to produce negative as well as positive results – the reason why, for example, one man is a success, and another is a failure. The difference between them lies in their minds. Similarly, why is one woman slim and another obese? You guessed it – they use their minds differently.

There are many powerful ways in which you can use your imagination to encourage change, and we'll look at these a little later in the book.

YOUR IMAGINATION CONTROLS YOUR FUTURE

It is truly amazing to learn that we can use our imagination to change the future. Social psychologists have found that when we imagine a certain outcome, it's more likely to happen than if we don't. It has been shown that when people imagine themselves achieving something, they tend to believe they can achieve it. We spend much of our time imagining future events. We are constantly seeing ourselves carrying out actions that are future-orientated. So, just as the golfer or the guy on the first date can envision and imagine a positive experience, we can use our imaginations to produce a satisfying and positive outcome for anything we do in our lives.

POSITIVE HYPNOSIS

As we discussed earlier, hypnosis isn't something we undertake for 20 minutes every day and then just forget about. Sure, taking a 20-minute break every day is one of the best things you can do to work towards your goals; however, it is also important to realise that we are constantly reprogramming ourselves with our self-talk. Words create images in our minds, and when we add emotion to the mix we are creating new 'programmes'.

When you have developed an understanding of the way your mind functions you will have greater awareness of how your thoughts and self-talk affect your daily life. You can begin to use hypnosis as you walk, while sitting in your car, at the gym or at the office, and you'll start to think in a new way. You'll begin to feel more relaxed and calmer, and you will have a more positive outlook on life in general. You will become more aware of your mind/body signals. Best of all, you will be silently and privately changing negative beliefs and behaviours about yourself. You will, in fact, go beyond positive thinking.

And underpinning all of this is a secret that you might not be aware of: *All hypnosis is self-hypnosis.* As your hypnotherapist I would offer your subconscious mind a set of ideas and suggestions. You, as my client, will accept these suggestions if they match your map of the world. If they don't they will be ignored, nothing much happens, and they have no real power. A good hypnotherapist is like a coach or a cheerleader. It is, however, you out there on the pitch playing your own game. This is not to say that you don't need the help of a good hypnotherapist, but the power of the hypnotist lies in his or her skill in using creative hypnotic techniques and good psychology.

It's not true that the hypnotist has any power over you, and neither should he or she. You are responsible for your own behaviour; you are your own master. You can create many changes yourself, when you know how.

HYPNOSIS VS MEDITATION

You don't have to choose between self-hypnosis and meditation. In fact, over the years I have found that they have much in common. When people choose to meditate, they usually want to improve their health, get in touch with their spirituality, or manage stress. These are all good things, and all forms of meditation are helpful in their pursuit. Many approaches to meditation offer a philosophy or a belief system, which some find appealing; however, when we practise self-hypnosis, we can *choose* what area of our lives we want to work on. We can create a programme that is right for us – whether it is developing our self-awareness, losing weight, achieving financial success, giving up smoking, or anything else we really want to achieve.

Both hypnosis and meditation offer a calm, peaceful, subjective state – a state in which we are open to new ideas and suggestions. Both are good and both can change your life. I teach a combination of hypnosis and meditation to my clients because they both offer powerful benefits. Whether you choose to practise meditation or hypnosis you are experiencing a natural trance state. And it is in this state that you open your mind to change.

THE LAW OF REVERSED EFFORT

This 'law of the mind' is useful to understand, for many reasons. The law of reversed effort simply means that the harder you try to do something, the more difficult it becomes. Does that seem to be something of an anomaly? Let's look at an example. Have you ever tried very hard to stick to a diet only to find that it becomes more and more difficult? We normally give up at this point, and revert to our old habits.

In my hypnosis work I sometimes encourage people to do an experiment. I ask them to close their eyes and imagine they can't open them. I tell them that after I have counted from one to five, to try and open their eyes. Most people find they can't after trying for a few moments. This is called the law of reversed effort. Remember the more you try to make something happen, the more difficult it seems to be. A good example is someone who has trouble sleeping, the more he tries to go to sleep, the more he stays awake. The best thing to do when you cant sleep is to try and stay awake, then you usually fall asleep. This is the law of reversed effort in action.

Exercise
Sit or lie down, relax, and tune into your breathing. In your mind slowly scan your body from the top of your head

down to the tips of your toes. Slowly tense and release each muscle as you work down your body. Take your time: gently tense and release the muscles in your face and head. Slowly move down into your neck and shoulders, your arms, legs, abdomen, chest and buttocks.

Now gently bring your awareness into your breathing as you continue to relax. Begin to focus on your eyelids. Imagine your eyelids are so relaxed, they just won't work. Imagine you have no muscles in your eyelids. Now tell yourself: 'My eyelids are stuck down, tightly shut, and I can't open them.' Tell yourself: 'The more I try, the more I can't ...'

You will be surprised to find your eyelids do not open; this is because you are using the word *try*. You may notice that if you replace the word *try* with *I can*, then you *can*. If you choose to open them by using the word *I can*, just allow them to close down again and relax more deeply.

As you drift deeper into comfort, begin to wonder how you can creatively use this principle of *reversed effort* in other areas of your life. Allow images, words and thoughts to drift though your mind for a few minutes before returning back to full awareness again.

CHAPTER 2

THE LAW OF HYPNOTIC ATTRACTION

The greatest discovery of my generation is that man can alter his life simply by altering his attitude of mind.
WILLIAM JAMES

Hypnosis is not really about taking away pain and unhappiness; it's more about creating comfort, pleasure, happiness, health and success. Your mind can attract whatever you focus on, so if you focus on unhappiness and poverty, that's what you are likely to get.

Your imagination can be used like a magnet to bring what you want into your life. Some people like to think of this as a metaphysical concept – the 'law of attraction', a so-called 'universal law'. Some people choose to have a more scientific approach. In our brain we have something called the 'reticular activating system'. This is the part of the brain that filters out certain people and things, leaving only the things and the people that we are interested in attracting. And it works. The important question is: What and who do you want to attract into your life? It's your choice, so what do you desire?

I believe that one of the reasons why people attract

problems in life is because they are stuck. They don't know how to move forward. When we look at how people change, we can see that it usually comes from doing something different. An alcoholic may cure himself by changing his friends or taking up a fitness programme. A smoker may just quit cigarettes because they meet a soulmate. An overweight woman might take a new job, and feel so much more confident and better in herself that she is inspired to lose weight. I see this type of thing all the time. One small change can, and does, lead to bigger changes.

What does this have to do with attracting things into our lives? Well, here's a secret: *You become what you think about all day*. These words are pure gold. There is no proof that the law of attraction actually exists (in a scientific way, i.e. like the law of gravity), but like does attract like. Look around you: successful people tend to hang out together, as do people who are out of work. Smokers commune with the smokers; idealists hang out with their idealistic mates, while the fitness buffs hit the gym together.

So the question is: *How can you take advantage of the law of attraction*? Well, one thing you can do is to spend your time with people who are successful in the area in which you want to be successful. Maybe you want to become fitter and healthier, so aim to spend some time with people who make it a priority. Perhaps you want to quit drinking alcohol, in which case a teetotal crowd is your best bet. If you want to be rich, then spend more time with people who have money. This is what I call the 'law of *hypnotic* attraction'. We are being influenced all the time by the people who we choose to be around, whether they are friends, acquaintances, spouses or work colleagues. This is not to say you should divorce your wife or husband or disown your friends; you just need to be aware of this hypnotic influence that people have on you – both good and bad.

One thing is for certain: if you spend a lot of time with negative people, you will find that achieving your goals and aspirations is that much more difficult! These people are everywhere – complaining about the weather, complaining about the boss, complaining about their lot in life – and they are people who actively look for reasons to whinge. You are different to these people; if you weren't you probably wouldn't be reading this book.

In a nutshell, if you hang out with losers you will become a loser. If you hang around winners you become a winner. Finding out who the winners are and who the losers are is now part of your job. Winners do not have to be wealthy, but they do need to have a positive outlook on life. What's a winner to you?

TIP
Don't walk away from negative people – *run*!

Attitude is everything. Spend time with people who have a good attitude, and life seems so much easier. One mistake business owners make is to employ people with a bad attitude; I know, I have done it myself many times. Once I discovered this secret my life suddenly got a whole lot easier. I believe this is the same in all relationships we have in life. And it's also important to check our own attitudes as well. Are we displaying a positive attitude to ourselves as well as to others? Reality check!

Remember you can use your mind to succeed in life, or you can use it to fail in life. It's up to you.

WHAT IS SUCCESS?

You and me, we want to be successful. We want to be able to achieve certain things in life. We are, after all, goal-directed beings. But let's clarify what we mean by success. Many people think of success in financial terms: in other words, someone is successful if they have achieved financial freedom. This is a number-one goal for some people. We live in a world that is driven by money and material possessions. But can we be successful with money alone? Unlikely, through many try. This is not because money is the root of all evil – far from it. It's because money plays a role in success and happiness, but it's not everything. We need balance in our lives, and that balance comes from something more than money.

I work every day with people who want to be successful – they want to be successful in controlling their anxiety or stress; they want to be successful at freeing themselves from smoking or being overweight. For most of us these are not easy things to achieve.

We are programmed from an early age to think in a certain way. We are taught that life is difficult; we are told we have to be grateful for what we get in life; and we are encouraged to watch and learn from our parents. We grow up wired with the beliefs and attitudes of our parents, and much of our present self-image is a result of our early programming. And yet, despite the fact that we have been programmed to think and behave in certain ways, we do seem to expect to be able to change our habits and behaviours overnight. The truth is that we need to unravel some of the programming and reprogramme it instead. We can certainly change habits and behaviours, but it requires work.

In reality, this is the essence of success – a constant commitment to change and personal growth. Why? Because every single time we make changes in our life we become more successful.

Think about the people you know who are jealous of others who have achieved financial success. Think about the people who are jealous of people who manage to change something about themselves, by changing the way they operate – their habits and behaviours, for example. But everything that others achieve is possible for us too. We can choose to design the life we desire through our own efforts. We are envious of people who can change their lives because we cannot see how easy it is to do it ourselves. We are envious because they seem to have something in them that we'll never have. But this is about as far from the reality as it's possible to be.

You are reading this book because there is some part of you that wants to change something in your life, something that will make you a more successful human being. Each time you make a change you alter your self-image. When you alter your self-image you feel better about yourself and the quality of your life improves. Little changes lead to bigger changes and success is, and can be measured, by achieving little goals along the way.

WHOSE LIFE IS IT ANYWAY?

If I told you that there's a good chance you aren't running your own life you might think I am just some kind of New-Age nut. But hear me out: we are all influenced by the people we choose to have around us. I say 'choose' because, like almost everything in life, we have a choice. A simple way of looking at things is like this: you want to quit smoking, everybody around you smokes, so, effectively, everybody is trying to get you to smoke a cigarette. It may not be a conscious manoeuvre on their part, but by lighting up themselves, they are persuading you to do the same. But it can be conscious, too. A smoker feels better if someone else is smoking, so they use a little influence to get you smoking too.

The same goes if you are trying to lose a few pounds. No one wants to indulge alone, so if you are sharing company with someone bound and determined to eat some chocolate, you can bet you'll be on the receiving end of some nudging to join him or her.

So what's happening here? Are we being reactive to someone else's desires? The truth is: *yes*. Behaviours are programmed into our brains and it doesn't take much to respond to things that encourage those behaviours. Think, for example, about a time when you set out to achieve something – maybe trying to write a book, or start a new business. One or more people may have expressed surprise and disapproval: *What? You want to start a business in a recession? Or do you know how many books are published each year? Why do you think you are different or special?* You hear a little voice inside your head: *Hmmm, what if they are right? Maybe I had better not take the risk; I might look a fool!*

When you learn the secrets of hypnosis, you can become proactive rather than reactive, and reframe these negative suggestions. You can programme your mind to design a life of happiness and success.

BECOME A SOURCE OF ENERGY

Einstein once said that you can't make energy and you can't destroy it – you can only transform it.

Each and every one of us is made up of energy, as is everything around us. What most people are not aware of is that we have the ability to change that energy. I am not talking about anything strange or mystical here; I am talking about changing the way we feel inside ourselves. The words we use have a powerful effect upon us, and upon those around us. Words have the ability to alter energy from being slow, negative and stagnant, to being powerful, vibrant and positive force for the good.

Think about the words you choose when communicating to others, and the *way* you communicate them. With positive words, and a smile on your face, you ignite energy. Frown, mumble and come out with negative words, and you drag everyone down – including yourself. This is the manipulation of energy in action.

Take me, for example. When I am asked how I'm feeling, I usually reply: 'I'm wonderful, thanks!'

This often takes people aback. On the surface this may seem like a polite reply, but the truth is that I am communicating emotion through my words. What gives you the best feeling: I'm *ok* or I'm *wonderful*? The more positively emotional your words, the better it makes the people to whom you are communicating feel, and the better you'll feel yourself.

Try it and see for yourself. Notice the response of the asker, and become aware of how you are feeling as well. And remember to smile: smiling is a universal language, wherever you are in the world. It has the instant effect of transmitting positive energy, which ripples outwards into the world. Try smiling at someone in the street, and take note of their surprised, but pleased response. Watch them – you may find they pass on the smile. Why? Because it's positive and it lifts spirits.

There are plenty of other words you can use to communicate how you feel. Think:

- amazing
- fantastic
- incredible
- exceptional
- sensational
- tremendous
- awesome
- phenomenal.

CHAPTER 3

THE SECRET OF HAPPINESS

Happiness depends upon ourselves.
ARISTOTLE

Happiness, like the concept of success, is subjective; that is, it varies between people and their perceptions. What is interesting, however, is that these 'perceptions' are often skewed in unhealthy directions, and we begin to look for success – and happiness – in all the wrong places.

What is happiness to you? Is it having a bigger car, a bigger house, or a better partner? The truth is that many people *have* got the bigger house, the bigger car and the better partner. Are they happy now? Maybe – though most are not. You see, happiness has nothing to do with having more material possessions.

So what is happiness? Happiness is, really, just good feelings – nothing more and nothing less. There is nothing or no-one on this planet that can make you happy, because real happiness comes from within. What appears to be 'finding happiness' is more about 'finding ourselves'. There is nothing wrong with achieving goals in life, nor is there anything wrong with wanting to better our lives. We are programmed to be goal-directed beings. We have to participate in the game of life. That's part of the reason we are here. But, equally, there are countless examples of people who appear to have everything but, in reality, have nothing. Why? Because they are not truly happy. If we look more closely at the question of happiness, we can see the evidence of unhappiness through the number of people struggling with addictions, depression and stress-related problems.

We must always strive for the things we *want* to do. We deserve to choose to be in the line of work that is right for our personality and character. Our life will flow more easily and naturally if we are with a partner who shares similar values and attitudes. We may feel more comfortable in a larger home, and have some fun with a new car. The true essence of happiness, however, lies within.

In Buddhism we are taught that desire creates suffering. This is undoubtedly true. Desire can and does create anxiety and distress. We all tend to island hop! We are constantly trying to move towards things that we don't – or even can't – have, which is a source of frustration, dissatisfaction and tension. And, of course, if we do manage to meet our desires, we experience fleeting happiness and then move on to the next goal. Chasing dreams can distract us from finding happiness where it truly can be found: within ourselves.

So how do we change? How do we become happier? First of all, we have to become aware of ourselves. We need to get to know ourselves better. The more we use alcohol and junk food to blot out the reality of our daily lives, the less likely it is that we will be able to see into the depths of ourselves and find out what is within. We'll be less likely to make good decisions and commitments, and we'll move further and further away from the happiness we all seek and deserve.

Imagine you have the power to change your inner state

and feel happy. Well you do! I am serious. You really can train your mind to be happier.

When you learn to take control of your mind, you learn to take control of your life.

NO-ONE IS COMING TO RESCUE YOU!

It's a funny state of affairs and common to all of us: when things get bad, we tend to pull into our shells and think that somehow, something – fate or some other divine intervention – will come to our rescue. It can take months or even years before we realise that no one is coming to save us. We gradually realise that only we have the power to change our situation, and in the time it has taken for us to come to this all-important conclusion, we have wasted precious time waiting for nothing to come.

Relying on ourselves doesn't mean that we can't or shouldn't seek help from time to time, as support, guidance and professional advice can be invaluable. What I mean is that action and change has to be driven by ourselves. It is our responsibility to get our lives back in check.

We can blame others, we can blame the environment or anything else, but ultimately we are completely responsible for ourselves, our lives and our actions. Some people will do everything in their power to avoid blaming themselves and accepting responsibility, but the buck stops here.

So, start to take responsibility for your life goals: your happiness, health and success. It is *you* who has to eat less and exercise more. It is *you* who has to accept that smoking is slowly killing you. It is *you* who has to take the risk and start that new business you have been dreaming about. And it is *you* who has to believe that change is possible for change to come. Change that only *you* can make.

YOUR MIND CAN KEEP YOU YOUNG

Your mind plays a big part in helping you to look and feel younger. Don't fall for the old 'it's genetics' line, which puts the onus and responsibility for your health and wellbeing firmly on to someone else's shoulders. Sure, genetics plays a small role in the way we age; however, it is positive living that encourages us to look and feel younger, and that starts with positive thinking.

I have a friend who believes that because he is over 40 and married, he must dress a certain way and frequent different types of places from the ones he used to visit. His attitude has become limited by preconceived ideas about what age and, in particular, being 40 and married, means.

Do you know anyone who thinks and behaves like an 'older person', just because he or she has reached a certain age? What about your attitude? Have you chosen to believe that at a certain point in your life you have to become something different – something that is recognised as being 'appropriate'? All of us change as we mature, but this is an organic, gradual process, and it does not have anything to do with changing in response to other people's expectations. It has to do with evolving – and we can maintain a positive attitude towards life as we do so.

And there's more.

PLAN TO RETIRE – OR PLAN TO DIE

I'm always amazed by the number of people who invest lots of energy in planning their retirement. I'm not suggesting you shouldn't plan for the future – far from it. What I'm saying is that you should not ever *retire*. Huh? I hear you asking.

Yes, I am serious. When people retire, they really are planning for death. Not consciously, of course; retirement is, however, planning for death. In his excellent book, *How To Turn Words into Money*, Ted Nicholas writes that Americans who retire at age 65 live an average of 17 months, whereas those who continue working live an average of 19 more years. That's quite a difference.

When people retire they tend to lose some of their self-esteem. We all desire to feel wanted and needed, and giving up a central feature of our lives that provides this can have an extremely negative effect. So give up the idea of retiring – you don't have to continue in the job you've been in for years, but you do need to keep on working at something you love – something that stimulates your mind and rewards you. Not only will you feel younger and more vibrant, but you'll also feel valued, which helps to keep self-esteem at healthy levels.

Consider charity work, or maybe turn a hobby into a small business. Write a book? They say there's a good book inside all of us – what about yours? And if you weren't fortunate to discover something you loved when you were younger, perhaps you can later in life. Remember, when you choose not to retire you may also be choosing a longer life. What's more, 'non-retirement' may provide you with the impetus for change that you've always wanted.

DO YOU SEE YOURSELF AS 'YOUTHFUL' AND 'BEAUTIFUL'?

There are millions of people all around the world spending vast sums of money on cosmetic surgery. Many of these people are obsessed with trying to make themselves *feel* good by changing their appearance. What these people don't realise is that no amount of money is going to change the fundamental problem. These people simply don't feel good about themselves.

One of the early pioneers of self-image psychology, Dr Maxwell Maltz, a professor of plastic surgery at the University of Nicaragua, found that not all of his patients felt better about themselves after surgery – even when the physical change was a great success and matched their wishes. This led Dr Maltz to investigate the concept of self-image, which proved to play a key role. When a person improves his or her self-image, the way they feel completely changes. This has nothing to do with appearance. Obviously we can feel depressed and disheartened when we feel we don't look our best – when we've put on too much weight, or burned the candle at both ends for too many nights on the trot – and this can definitely act as an impetus to make some changes towards health and wellbeing. However, if our self-image becomes dependent upon the way we look, we will never attain true happiness. Not one of us is perfect, and involving ourselves in a search for elusive perfection or beauty is only going to lead to disappointment. It's rather like the Buddhist approach to desire – we may experience fleeting happiness when we get something we want but that happiness will be short-lived as we set our sights higher and higher.

When working with clients who want to lose weight I've noticed that they often find they don't need to lose as much as they thought they did. This is because I helped them to change their self-image. As a result, they felt better about themselves, and both looked *and* felt great. Change comes from within, and change also affects what is within.

Exercise

This is a good exercise to remind ourselves that happiness is just good feelings!

Close your eyes and tune into the most comfortable part of yourself. Imagine a time, back in your past, when you felt the happiest you can remember. Picture the image in your mind. Make it big, bright and colourful. Now step into the image and connect with those happy feelings. Take some time to tune into the sensations, see what you saw, feel what you felt and hear what you heard.

Now, through your own eyes, look out of the image and see yourself at the age you are now. See the image in front of you. Imagine yourself floating forward into the image, bringing all those past feelings of happiness with you. Repeat this exercise until you can feel the positive feelings inside you.

You may need to practise this exercise for several days until you merge the happy feelings into the present you.

CHAPTER 4

THE POWER OF BELIEFS

They are because they think they are.
VIRGIL

Much of what you have in your life right now is the
result of what you have learned to believe. There was
a time when you came to believe you could do the job that
you do now. There was a time when you believed that you
could earn the income that you are earning now. Any
stress-related problem you have ever had manifested from
what you chose to believe. Beliefs are powerful: they can
create miracles and they can create illness, or even death.
They can move us forward, or they can stop us in our
tracks. They can gear us up to go for a new job, or prevent
us from trying anything new.

Most of our core beliefs come from our parents. As
children we had to look to our parents to learn what was
right and wrong. We can think of our parents as being two
giant hypnotists who filled our minds with ideas and
suggestions – some of which were good and some of which
were bad. What we were taught by our parents did, to a
large degree, make us the person we think we are. For
example, if your parents told you that you were a
wonderfully gifted and talented child, there is a strong
chance that you have grown up to be a confident and self-
assured adult. If your parents told you that you were

stupid, you'd be more likely to grow up clumsy and lacking in confidence. Your parents may have encouraged you to believe that everything is worth a try, and that the world is your oyster, or they may have been overly cautious and discouraged you from stepping outside the 'safe' and 'known'. They may have trusted you and afforded you responsibility, giving you wings to soar, or they may have clipped your wings and forced you to live by other people's rules, making you less likely to try new things as an adult.

Our beliefs guide and direct our lives, and the power of believing has been known since the dawn of time. Probably the most powerful example of this concept in action is voodoo. Voodoo is a religion, based pretty much on superstition. It works on the power of belief, and is very real to the cultures that were brought up to believe in it. Even now it is practised in some parts of the world, such as Haiti. One of the compelling elements of voodoo is that it has the power to heal and to hurt, and that spirits and their worldly priests have the power to cause death and destruction, as well as health, happiness and even love.

The same goes for witch doctors from aboriginal tribes in Australia. If a witch doctor points a bone at another person with the intention of placing a curse upon him or her, chances are the victim will respond to that curse. Why? Because the belief system is so strong, the curse is physically manifested, and the victim becomes ill or even dies as a result of this belief. Beliefs are powerful, and they can be used positively or negatively.

Think of beliefs as being a generator for your behaviours. When you change a belief you automatically change your behaviour.

HOW WE CREATE OUR PROBLEMS

Many people believe that problems (such as losing a job, a divorce, dire financial straits, etc.) are the cause of depression, anxiety, addictions and phobias. While this may appear to be the case on the surface, this belief is nothing but an illusion. Let me give you an example:

A man called Sam suffers depression because his wife walks out on him, or so he thinks. If that was true, every man who has had a wife leave him would get depressed. In reality, the beliefs that Sam formed when his wife left him created the depression. End of story.

It works like this: Event – Belief – Outcome.

Let's take this a little further. Jane loses her job, and she forms a belief: I am no good; I am useless: I will never find another job. Jane becomes depressed. Jane has created or accepted a negative belief after losing her job, and it guides her future.

Now look at John. John's wife leaves him, and John jumps for joy. Hurray! Now he can find someone who truly loves him!

And Susan is made redundant. She jumps for joy! Hurray! Now she can take a break, find a better job and make more money.

Both John and Susan created positive beliefs after what many people would perceive to be a negative event. And, as a result, their future looks much brighter than Jane and Sam's did.

It is not what happens to us that creates the problems; in other words, it is not the 'event'. It is what we *do with the experience* that makes the difference. Sometimes we can look back to a past experience, which seemed horrific at the time, and realise that it was, in fact, a good and positive thing. Since the event, we have formed positive new beliefs and literally reframed the whole experience.

We can do that now, in response to any event in our lives. We simply have to find the 'silver lining', see the positive, and then focus on believing it.

Exercise

1. Write down a recent event that has left you feeling a little depressed, anxious or angry.

2. Write down the beliefs you hold about that past event.

3. Now, think about how awful and terrible it was.

4. Next, think about how you can turn it into a positive. For example, what have you learned from this experience that could help you in the future? Has it freed you to do something else with your life? Has it shocked you into making changes you had been reluctant or too lazy to make? Ask yourself what positives there are.

5. Now consider how to find ways to change your beliefs about the event. Close your eyes and go inside. Allow yourself to be comfortably relaxed. Have an inner dialogue with the part of you that thinks it's awful and the part of you that can see, and feel some positive side to it. Look at it from many different angles. Focus on how you can work it to your advantage. Work at putting it in a new, more positive frame.

With desire and a little work you may be surprised how your beliefs begin to change.

LETTING GO OF FEAR

Why do people get into difficulties? In almost all cases fear is at the root. It's absolutely essential that you take this concept on board, because it may well be the single thing that is holding you back from making the changes you want or need in your life. We can fear many things – for example, we may be afraid of:

- criticism
- rejection
- failure
- being unloved
- sickness
- dying
- success.

These are probably the most common of human fears, and there are undoubtedly more. When we are paralysed by fear our lives become limited. One of the most common fears is fear of criticism. Being controlled by this fear can be almost as crippling as being physically paralysed. Why? Because fear of criticism can destroy your dreams and life goals. This fear can make sure that we never risk anything. And by risking nothing, we *become* nothing and *are* nothing.

This may sound like a strong statement, and it most definitely is. What's more, it is very true. Being reactive to fears produces a mediocre life, because we create boundaries that confine, ensnare and control us, and fears prohibit change. All change carries with it some risk, and if we become fearful of taking risks for fear of 'criticism', 'rejection', 'failure' or anything else on the list above, we simply cannot change.

We are here to be the best we can be, and the reason why so few people reach their true potential is largely down to the fact that they are afraid. Think of the times that you have put off doing something you really wanted to do: start a new business, get out of an unhappy relationship, or write that book. What stopped you? Fear. Think about it.

The first step to eliminating these fears is awareness. When we learn to tune into these fears, we can actually hear our negative self-talk, and we can put a stop to it. Every single time we hold back from doing something we want to do – hold back from making changes or moving forward in our lives – stop and think: *What am I afraid of?* When you've got some answers to that question, it's time to work through those fears and banish them once and for all. We can begin by being more proactive – working to change our limiting beliefs, the ones that keep us stuck firmly in our comfort zone. We can also change our mental chatter and self-talk to something more positive.

Exercise

Put yourself into a comfortable relaxed state (see page 83). As you relax deeply, tune into what it is you are putting off, or procrastinating about. As you relax notice what thoughts, words or images come up. Pay attention to your internal dialogue. What are you telling yourself that is keeping you fearful? You may not get it at first. Just keep with it as you continue to expand your awareness.

CHAPTER 5

THE POWER OF SELF-TALK

All that we are is the result of what we have thought.
The mind is everything. What we think we become.
BUDDHA

What does your self-image say to you? Each and every one of us holds a mental blueprint in our subconscious mind – a blueprint that represents our self-image. It is not 'who we are' but 'who we think we are'. Our self-image is, in reality, the sum total of the thoughts and beliefs we hold about ourselves. So, people who have trouble with their weight often have a self-image that says things like: 'I love junk food', 'exercise is boring', 'I'm not the sporty type', 'being overweight is in my genes', and so on.

People who suffer from low confidence have a self-image that says: 'I doubt myself', 'I'm not worthy of great things', 'I am not capable of doing this', 'the other guy is better than me', and so on.

Basically, you can try all you like to 'outwit' your self-image– by using will power, or making a concerted effort to get what you want; however, if you want long-lasting change that self-image has to shift completely. And you *can* change your self-image. You *do* have the power to create a new mental blueprint of yourself, based on what you want to become.

Obviously it's difficult to create a new mental blueprint if you aren't sure what the old one looks like. To become aware of your inner blueprint, or your self-image, you must become aware of yourself. You must make yourself the subject of contemplation and study – study your attitudes and your goals. What do you have in your life at this time? This can be a clue to the way you see yourself. What is the state of your health and fitness, your finances, your relationships? All of these will tell you something about yourself.

If you could think of five or 10 words or phrases to describe yourself, what would they be? These words will also help to form a picture of the blueprint you are carrying with you. Think of a few negative or positive experiences that you've had in the past. What were your feelings about yourself afterwards? Did you lose your job and think, 'I'm worthless' or did you think 'I'm better off without them'? Did you blame someone else, or take responsibility yourself? Did you learn something from the experience, or close yet another door? Your reactions to situations are an important part of your blueprint. Take note of them, to help build up the picture.

SELF-TALK: THE KEY TO A POSITIVE SELF-IMAGE

What you say to yourself on a regular basis can have a big impact on your self-image. If you are constantly telling yourself how confident you are, and if you imagine yourself acting in a confident way, you find you *do* start to act and feel more confident. Words create mental images in our mind, and repeating them has a way of burying them in our subconscious.

What images do you create in your mind? If you choose to create negative images through the use of negative language, you will find yourself with a negative experience of life. Negative words create negative images, which create negative feelings and experiences.

When we want to change, we need to reprogramme ourselves for success. And there are a few ways to do this.

First of all, we need to use the present tense. Our subconscious mind understands the present tense, so talk to your subconscious as though you have already become how you want to be. So, for example, you might say: 'I find I am relaxed and calm around people', 'I am feeling confident as I speak to a group' or I enjoy eating smaller portions of food, because I want to lose weight'. The present tense is powerful; it is the language of the subconscious.

WORDS ARE POWERFUL

There are some words that we all use out of habit – words that are literally hardwired into our nervous systems. These words can sabotage our life goals and should be avoided at all cost. Watch out for:

- *Trying*. The word 'try' suggests failure; it implies that something is going to be difficult to achieve. This perception is then communicated to your subconscious mind.
- *Not*. In other words, negative use of language, as in 'I will *not* eat chocolate any more'. This statement is a great example of focusing on precisely what you don't want to focus on! In other words, your subconscious is drawn to the word 'chocolate' and immediately forms

an image of it. Words should always focus on the images that you *do* want. So think instead, 'I choose to eat fresh fruit', and 'I enjoy eating fresh vegetables'.

- *Will.* When we use the word 'will', we are not communicating with the subconscious as well as we could, because we are not operating in the present. And as the old adage goes: tomorrow never comes! For this reason, even positive statements may not produce powerful results. So, instead of saying, 'I will exercise more' or 'I will smoke only 5 cigarettes a day', you'll say, 'I exercise more now' and 'I smoke 5 cigarettes a day'. Instead of 'I will be more confident when I speak to the group', it becomes 'I feel confident as I speak to the group'. When we use the word 'will', we are moving away from the present tense and, as a result, it has less hypnotic power.

- *Never.* Think about it! *Never* being able to eat a piece of chocolate or drink a glass of wine again? It's an absolute and there is no flexibility here. It is a final pronouncement, and it puts incredible pressure on us. It also works to get our backs up, because no one likes being told that they can 'never' do something again. Use the word never, and change may never happen!

- *Should.* This is another word that creates more anxiety than any other word I know. Again, there is no real flexibility in the word 'should', and it manages to create negative images that may make you shudder. For example, 'I should go on a diet' or 'I should relax more'. 'Shoulds' sound like instructions from our parents or teachers, and if there's anything that turns most of us off change, it's the idea that we have to do it, or we 'should' do it. The word 'should' also suggests that someone else thinks we should undertake a particular change. Change has to come from within. I recommend that you banish this word from your self-hypnosis and self-talk vocabulary.

- *Must.* Another word full of pressure, with no flexibility. Once again, none of us particularly likes being told what we have to do and the doors close the minute that word is uttered. 'I must not get nervous' or 'I must win this game' sounds like a challenge rather than a positive action, and for some reason, it doesn't actually seem achievable.
- *Can't.* Here is a word that we all take for granted, and it's just one letter away from being one of the most positive words on the planet. So remember, the next time you find yourself using the word 'can't', just lop off that 't', and then you can!

WORDS THAT CAN CHANGE YOUR LIFE

Just as negative words can undermine your efforts, and create a negative self-image in your subconscious, there are other, more positive words that can have a dramatic and powerful effect on your life. Use these words to design powerful self-suggestions to help you to create personal change.

- *Because*
  This is an interesting word, for lots of reasons. For example, in an experiment, social psychologist Ellen Langer proved that when we ask a favour of someone, we are likely to get a better response if we give a reason. Most surprisingly, it was discovered that the

best results came when the word *because* was used. So, instead of 'walking to the front of a supermarket queue asking can I pay for my groceries first', you might say 'Can I pay for my groceries first, because I've got a toddler waiting in the car'. Or 'Would you mind working an extra hour tonight, because I'm running very late'. A lot of this also has to do with our childhood conditioning. As a child you may remember almost pleading with your mother to let you have some more sweets. Remember this?

Child: Mummy, can I have some more sweets?
Mother: No, you can't.
Child: Mummy, please.
Mother: No
Child: Why not?
Mother: Because I said you can't!

As children we were usually given reasons in the form of a 'because' (even if they were rather unsatisfactory reasons, as in the above scenario) and, as a result, we expect and respond to the word because. It has been programmed into our subconscious mind. Maybe you can use the same technique to persuade yourself to make some changes. For example, 'I enjoy eating small amounts of food, because I want to get thin' or 'I enjoy freedom from tobacco, because I feel healthier'. You get the picture.

- *Now*
  The same thing goes here. Remember instructions from your parents, such as 'tidy your room *now*'? A lot of

things that our parents requested came in the form of 'orders' followed by a decisive 'now' or 'this second'. Not surprisingly, people respond well to it – one reason why hypnotherapists love to use the word! For example, 'Close your eyes, and relax *now* …'

- *Imagine*
  This is a word with true hypnotic power. *Imagine* how your life changes after you have read this book. *Imagine* being able to close your eyes and relax instantly. *Imagine* feeling totally confident talking to a large crowd. Your imagination creates images that are absorbed by your subconscious. Imagining things can help to make them happen.

You can make a habit of using these words as part of your self-hypnosis, with your eyes closed or open, without being in a relaxed state. They'll help to programme your subconscious mind. For example:

- I can *imagine* myself slim, *now*.
- I am confident when talking to groups of people, *because* I feel good about myself.
- I am *now* free from tobacco.
- I *imagine* myself wealthy *because* I choose to be successful.
- I choose to be healthy *because* I want to feel amazing.
- I can see myself at my ideal weight six months in the future, *now*.

As we discussed earlier, when you use positive self-talk, it's best to speak in the present tense. The subconscious mind only knows the present, even if you are talking about the future. One way of doing this is to add *now* at the end of each statement; for example, 'Next Thursday, I am feeling confident as I stand before the crowd *now*' or 'Next Thursday I am confident *now*'.

MORE WORD MAGIC ...

The 'even though' technique

The word 'but' is interesting because it tends to delete the statement that comes before it, and puts more emphasis on the words that come after. Here is a technique that changes the frame when you want to qualify something.

Think of a positive statement that uses the word 'but'. For example, 'I found the answer to my problem, but it could return again in the future.'

Change this to: 'I found the answer to my problem, even though it might return again in the future.'

See the difference?

Don't read this!

I knew you would! Why? Because what your brain was really hearing was the instruction involved – in other words, 'read this section'. Don't is an interesting word. As children we were often given instructions involving the word 'don't' and, of course, we 'did'. For example, 'Don't make a mess', 'Don't touch that' and 'Don't run'. Over the years our brain has learned to delete this word, and favour the words that come after it.

Now it is a powerful directive. Let me prove it! 'Don't think of a pink cat walking down the garden path'. What did you just think of? You did think of a pink cat because you had to – in order to get a representation of what was being requested. Here are some more. Don't:

- Think of the colour of your front door …
- Think of the colour of your car …
- Think of a white sandy beach …

You see my point, don't you?

Now you can understand why using the word 'don't' simply doesn't work. You say 'Don't eat chocolate', 'Don't get angry' or 'Don't forget to pick up the dry cleaning' and, of course, you *do.*

Here's a powerful way to use the word 'don't'. How about saying to yourself: 'Don't leave food on my plate' or 'Don't relax'. And, if you suffer from insomnia, what about 'Don't allow my eyelids to get heavy'.

Forget 'I can't' – say 'I won't'

I would like a pound coin for every time that someone has said to me: 'I can't': 'I can't stop eating sweets', 'I can't stop smoking' or 'I can't change'. It's amazing how people choose to reinforce their beliefs rather than change them. And, in reality, every time that you affirm this belief – every time you say you can't do something – you are right. If you continually tell yourself 'I can't change', then you won't change. So instead of saying 'I can't', start saying 'I won't'. Why? Because it's true, which is one step in the right direction. You are choosing not to change; change is not impossible.

The power of how

Have you ever asked yourself, 'Why, oh why …'? 'Why do I always raid the biscuit jar when I get home?' 'Why can't I be more assertive with the boss?' 'Why do I always get angry when someone cuts me up when I am driving?' Why-why-why? We ask ourselves why because we have been programmed to use this sort of language.

Now how about making a few changes to this approach. Instead of asking 'why', ask 'how'. So, 'How can I enjoy less food?' 'How can I be more assertive?' How can I be calmer when someone makes a mistake on the road?'

Imagine how using this approach will make a difference to you. The problem with the word 'why' is that it doesn't move to the solution. It simply means attempting to try to self-analyse and get to the bottom of things. When you ask 'how' you are actively opening your mind for solutions, rather than looking for causes. When you search for solutions, you have a better chance of finding one. You can also use this technique when you are communicating with others. It's almost always better to ask 'how' rather than 'why'. As the great family therapist Virginia Satir said, 'Asking "why" creates defence'. So how are you going to use this to help yourself?

MIND-ACCESSING QUESTIONS

Direct affirmations can be tough for your subconscious mind to digest if an inner conflict exists. For example, you might choose to say 'I am confident'. But then a little voice pipes up and says, 'Oh, no you're not'. What's the answer? You can, of course, create a 'choice affirmation' (see page 46), or you can direct a question to your subconscious. When we present our inner mind with a question, we send it on a deep, inner search. We are, in a sense, asking our subconscious for answers. This can be a much more powerful approach to lasting change. So when your inner voice starts saying 'I don't believe you', it's time to take a different approach, and this can begin by asking questions. For example:

- How can I feel confident?
- How can I enjoy smaller amounts of food?
- How can I feel calm?
- How can my inner healer help me to reduce my discomfort?
- I wonder how my inner mind can help me to become free from tobacco?
- I wonder how my subconscious mind can help me find a solution to this problem?
- I wonder how my subconscious mind can help me relax more easily?

Can you see the difference? How asking questions breaks down any resistance you might have? The first three 'how' questions are particularly powerful because they also include a direct affirmation – 'I feel confident', for example, or 'I enjoy smaller amounts of food'. And when we use the word 'wonder', we are encouraging our inner mind to search for solutions. This is also a very powerful approach to creating change.

THE POWER OF POST-HYPNOTIC SUGGESTIONS

Everything you suggest to yourself can be looked upon as a 'post-hypnotic' suggestion. What's that? Generally speaking, a post-hypnotic suggestion is a suggestion that is given during hypnosis for an action or response to take place after the hypnotic experience. So, during hypnosis, I might suggest to you that you are 'now free from tobacco', or that you are confident, or that you are committed to losing weight. These suggestions can be tremendously powerful, and form part of the basis of hypnotherapy.

What I am suggesting here is that you can give yourself post-hypnotic suggestions. For example, when you say to yourself that you are free from tobacco, you are feeding a suggestion into your mind, into your subconscious. Think about it: many of the things that occur in your life are the result of these self-suggestions. Example: I can see myself being nervous at my job interview today. So, how are you going to use the power of suggestion to your advantage?

By being aware of the words you choose you can literally change your life. You can now start to think about the many ways of using the right words in the right way, to help you create amazing changes in your life, starting today. This is going to take some work. You have got to increase your awareness to the point that you know the patterns of your thoughts. This is going to take some everyday mindfulness, and it's going to be well worth the effort.

Some of you may be thinking that this all sounds like too much work; but isn't it just as much work to run those old, negative thought patterns? Programming yourself for ill health, misery and financial hardship can take a lot more energy than creating more positive programmes.

The first thing you need to do is learn the art of relaxation, and then go on to work on your self-awareness. Then it's time to apply the power of hypnotic language. Let's get started.

CHAPTER 6

CHOICE: THE ANCESTOR OF CHANGE

*There is nobody who totally lacks the
courage to change.*
ROLLO MAY

It's been said that too much choice creates distress. While there is some truth to this we have to accept that choice is part of life. We make choices all the time: what to have for lunch, where to go on the weekend, what time to get up in the morning, and which train to take. We choose who we spend our lives with. Everything we do is effectively a choice we have made.

Beliefs are also a choice. Some of the choices we have made may have been formed at an unconscious level, but still they are choices. When we realise that we have choice in almost every area of our lives we give ourselves incredible power. I first discovered the power of choice through the writings of Dr Robert Anthony. In his superb book, *Beyond Positive Thinking*, Dr Anthony talks about how we can use the power of choice in our daily affirmations to create change.

When we choose to choose, something amazing happens to us. We sense that change is possible. The negative voice in our heads is silenced. Make a statement now inside your head – an affirmation that confirms how you want to be. For example, 'I feel confident'. Now listen to your inner critic. Is it telling you 'Who are you kidding – you can't even cold call a new prospect'? Or what about, 'I love healthy food'. 'Are you crazy,' says the inner critic, 'you had a cheeseburger yesterday'. After a while, it's no surprise that we start to listen to that negative, internal voice.

But what if you said to yourself, 'I *choose* to feel confident'? Notice how it feels when you say 'I choose'. When we put 'I choose' before an affirmation, the wall of resistance collapses; we feel empowered.

Here are some good examples of this type of approach in action:

- I choose to eat healthy, nutritious foods.
- I choose to feel confident as I stand before the crowd.
- I choose to be relaxed and comfortable.
- I choose to become wealthy and successful.
- I choose to create my own destiny.
- I choose to listen to my own intuition.
- I choose to learn from my mistakes.
- I choose to be happy.

Exercise
Now spend a few minutes creating some of your own 'I choose' statements.

THE POWER OF 'I AM'

A natural progression from I choose is 'I am'. When you start to hold the belief that you really can choose, it becomes easier to say 'I am'. And when you can say 'I am' and believe it without any self-doubt, you are in a very resourceful state. When you can use the affirmation 'I am' and believe it, *do it*. If you find a part of you disagrees, change to 'I choose'.

So:

- I am confident.
- I am relaxed.
- I am free from tobacco.
- I am successful.
- I am healthy.
- I am wonderful.
- I am amazing.

Exercise

Spend a few minutes experimenting with some of your own 'I am' statements.

CHOICE IN ACTION

Is your life the product of choice? Are you spending your life doing a job you love? Do you look forward to Monday morning? Maybe you do receive a lot of satisfaction from the work you do. The problem is that most people don't like their work, yet continue to spend most of their lives doing it. Are you reactive or are you pro-active? Are you living out *your* desires or someone else's?

To exercise the power of choice we need to be pro-active. When we are being reactive, we find ourselves being dragged through life following the goals and desires of others. We allow ourselves to be part of another person's plan; in a sense we give up some of our power. It's like stepping onto a stage and allowing ourselves to be influenced by the hypnotist.

There is nothing wrong with serving others. After all, that's part of the reason why we're here. There is also nothing wrong with working for other people. The point here is, is this *your* choice? We aren't here on this blue planet for long, so ask yourself: What do you want out of life?

It always amazes me when I hear people complaining about their work. I ask these people: 'Why not do something else?' They normally reply something along the lines of, 'It's all I know'. The reality is it's all they know up to that point in their lives. Life is a continuous journey till the day we die.

Sometimes people fear success. This isn't an active fear; rather, something that lurks at the subconscious level. Some people even unconsciously sabotage their success because they don't feel they deserve any. Their ego starts to trick them; their poor self-image comes springing back. For others it is a fear of failure. Again, this fear may be simmering away in your subconscious without giving you any clue or understanding of why you never meet your goals, and usually give up before you've even got partway there.

When we are crippled by fear we distort our future vision. How can we move forward in life when we continue to block our own paths? Yet this is what many people do.

This is your life and only you should choose how to live it

HOW TO TAKE ACTION IN LIFE

Sometimes change happens easily. Most of the time, it seems difficult. Why? Because everything you and I do on a regular basis is the product of repetition and the subconscious mind thrives on this. People fear change: in fact most are terrified of it. We are creatures of habit. This is a good thing in many ways; it's good for our health and wellbeing to have some structure in our lives.

Burn your bridges and change

One way of creating change is to burn your bridges. This is without a doubt the boldest approach to change that I know of, and also the most powerful.

Imagine you want to lose 30 pounds of fat. This would be a challenging task for almost anyone on the planet. What would happen if you told everyone you knew that if you didn't lose the weight by a certain date, you'd give £1,000 to a total stranger. Would you lose the 30 pounds? You probably would. This is what we call 'getting leverage', and you can apply this technique to most goals that you want to achieve.

Just think about what you want to achieve, and make sure there is a price to pay if you don't succeed. One way to do this is to advertise your goal to your friends and your family, or even place an ad in your local newspaper. Tell everyone you meet. If there is one thing that is common to most of us, it is a dislike of losing face. Most of us will meet our goals for fear of looking foolish.

A word of warning: make sure you are serious about making changes. If you think getting leverage will work even if you don't truly desire to make the change, think again. You may lose more than 'face'!

THERE IS NO SUCH THING AS FAILURE, ONLY FEEDBACK

I can remember a fellow hypnotist saying to me many years ago: 'You don't fail until you give up'. And the more I think about that statement, the truer it becomes. Taking this a step further, consider the words of a wealthy man, who once said: 'If you want to double your success rate, you have to double your failure rate first'.

Too many people who try to achieve things give up too soon. One reason for this is because we continually choose the same old methods when we attempt to achieve something. How can we expect to reach our goals when we continue to do things that simply don't work. Sometimes all we need to do is look to the obvious. If we 'failed', what can we learn from the experience? How can we do things differently next time?

Here is a simple example: A young man goes into the restaurant business and then goes bust after a year. The young man then tells himself that he's failed and never goes into business again. This man *has* failed, but for the sole reason that he *chose* to give up. Had he looked closely at his operation and assessed what hadn't worked, he might have learned from the experience and been able to start again. His first 'failure' could be written off as an important lesson, rather than being deemed something negative. It's interesting to note that most extremely successful people have had many, many failures before their successes, and often continue to make mistakes. There really is no such thing as overnight success. It's just that we don't often hear about the pain and struggle that goes on before.

The real secret to any kind of success is to keep going, making sure we continue to make the necessary adjustments along the way. This might mean making changes inside ourselves as well as outside.

A MODEL FOR CHANGE

The world is constantly changing, and our life experience is one of change. Imagine if nothing or no one ever changed. The planet would be a messed-up place, wouldn't it? On the other side of the coin, change can be uncomfortable and challenging.

I believe that all of us, deep down, want to improve some aspect of our lives. I also believe that we were put here on this earth to be the best we can be. I have found that the reason why people become stuck in their lives is because something needs to change. It might be a relationship that's not working, or perhaps a career that's no longer satisfying. Maybe a change in lifestyle is needed. Whatever it is, action will eventually be needed in order to create change. Here is how the process of change works:

1. In your current state of being, you become aware that a change is needed
2. Your level of pain or discomfort in your current state increases.
3. You begin to move toward the desired change.
4. You experience a form of chaos as you move through this process of change.
5. You find yourself integrating new learning.
6. You experience a new positive state of being.

This is the process involved in any major change you have experienced in your life. And you will experience the same in other new and future changes. You can make the process of change easier when you use hypnosis to assist you.

THE 'TADIN' PRINCIPLE

The great American psychologist William James once said, 'Man's greatest fear is change'. And if we look around us, the truth of this statement becomes increasingly clear. People stay in jobs they hate, they fester in unhealthy relationships, and continue habits and behaviours that are slowly destroying their health. So how can we change, and stay changed?

We take action!

Let's suppose you want to quit smoking. The first thing you have to do is make the decision to stop. Once that decision is made it's time to take action. Make a date, tell everyone about it, and start to work on the change.

So to begin with, we need to *think*: think about what is required to make the change. We need a strategy, and when we have that strategy we need to take action. The faster we act the faster our brain begins the process of change. This isn't rocket science, but it's important. The biggest challenge for most people seems to be the 'act' of taking action. There are many possible reasons for this, and fear is the biggest one (see page 31).

What's the secret? TADIN? *Think And Do It Now*, of course. This is good advice. *Think and do it now.*

ACT AS IF YOU CAN

When clients say to me, 'I wish I was a success', I always say, 'But you are!'

'But I'm not,' they protest, to which I respond, 'Well, pretend you are'.

There are times in life when we have to change fast, and one of the best ways to create rapid change is to act out the changes; in other words, think about what it is you want to change, and then act as if you *have* changed. This works particularly well for developing self-confidence, motivation and assertiveness. Imagine, for example, that you want be more assertive around certain people. You can begin by watching people who *are* assertive and modelling them. One of the fastest ways to learn how to do something is to watch someone doing it. Some of the latest research in neuroscience shows when we watch people performing behaviours our brain replays them back. And for many years, watching people performing their skills has been a large part of the learning process. So the next time you have to change something quickly, just pretend you already have changed!

CHAPTER 7

CHANGING YOUR MIND

Change always comes bearing gifts.
PRICE PRITCHETT

Exercise

Want to change a habit quickly? Although change can be slow, even painful at times, it can also be surprisingly fast and easy. Everyone knows someone who has changed almost overnight. Perhaps they have suddenly stopped smoking or quit chocolate. Maybe they have given up the need to procrastinate. In most cases this is due to the fact that the person is at a point in their lives when they are ready to change.

If you feel that you are close to making a decision to change a negative habit, this technique may be the just the help you need. I like to call this the 'switch-swop' pattern.

Sit down, close your eyes and allow yourself to relax. Imagine yourself just about to do the habit you don't want to do. Put yourself in the situation, as if you are there – for example, bringing a cigarette up to your mouth, in a situation where you are about to procrastinate, staring at your accounts, eating chocolate, or whatever.

As you do this, see what you see, hear what you hear, and feel what you feel. Become aware of any tastes or smells, if appropriate. Make sure you get a good representation of the habit and your surroundings.

Now put this image to one side for a moment. Create another image of yourself, as you want to become, knowing that you are free of this habit. Maybe you can remember a time in your life when you were fully in control and free of this habit.

As you construct the image, make sure you feel compelled to move toward what you see, hear, feel, taste and smell.

Now add one more thing. Think of all the people who you love and admire. Put them in this new image, see their smiling faces, see and hear them cheering for the new you, feel their love and support.

When you are happy with this new image, put a frame around it, using the most positive colour you can think of – a colour that fits this new you.

Now bring back the negative image. Imagine the new positive image directly in front of you, maybe in your hand or somewhere else in the middle of the negative image.

Make sure you have a good representation of both images. As you focus on the two images, slowly count backwards from 10 to one. When you get to one, *as quickly as you can,* shrink the negative image down to the size of a dot and send it into the distance. At the same time, blow up the new image. Make it big and bright. See yourself standing out in front of you, with your friends and loved ones cheering you on, knowing you are now free from the old habit you once had.

Repeat the process of swapping the images 5 to 10 times. Do it *fast!*

Now you are going to find it difficult to get the old negative picture back. If not, repeat the process.

Many people find that after doing this 5 to 10 times, the

habit is gone! Others find that they may have to practise it a few more times. For best results repeat this exercise 5 times each day for 5 days, to reinforce the change.

ANCHOR IT

You may have heard about the famous scientist, Ivan Pavlov. In his well-known experiment with dogs, Pavlov would ring a bell when it was the dogs' feeding time. After he repeated this exercise several times, the dogs salivated at the sound of the bell. This is called a 'conditioned reflex', or an 'anchor'. We are all surrounded by these anchors. As an example, hearing a certain song or going to a certain place might remind you of a certain person or a certain time. If I say to you, 'Just do it!' what brand of shoe do you think of?

These associations are all around us – places that remind us of good times, films that relate to people we have spent time with, photographs, songs – and all of these can be anchors that evoke feelings and memories. You can also create your own anchors by using your mind. When you programme your own mind to experience a feeling, you can access this state any time you choose to. Anchors can be created by touch, sound or an image. The best way to programme feel good anchors is by touch. When we associate a feeling or memory with a specific physical touch we can put ourselves back into that state quickly and easily.

Exercise

Try this exercise now. Close your eyes and relax, really relax, and tune into the comfort inside your body. As you become more and more comfortable, allow your mind to drift back to a time when you felt really relaxed and free of any stress and tension. Notice how you felt, what you saw around you and what you heard. Allow the feelings to spread and deepen. As the feelings intensify, gently hug your right wrist with your left hand. Make sure the feelings of comfort are strong, as you gently squeeze your wrist. Now relax your hands and let your mind clear.

Now gently squeeze your wrist and notice the feelings of comfort and relaxation coming back to you. To reinforce this anchor, repeat it each day.

BACK TO THE FUTURE: THE MAGIC QUESTION

The great hypnotherapist Milton Erickson said that we should spend our lives with one foot in the future and one foot here in the present. This makes good sense and my personal experience with clients backs this up. Too many people spend too much time with one foot in the future and one foot in the past.

This way of thinking and being leads to anxiety and stress. In a perfect world, we would always stay in the present – the 'here and now'. But this is, of course, unrealistic. What's more, our past holds a treasure trove of learnings and resources that can be useful to us now.

But hold on there. Maybe our past – with its successes and mistakes – doesn't always hold the answers to our problems. Some good, recent research has found that the future may hold more solutions to our problems than the past. Most of this research has been done in the area of depression. One major thing that people with depression share is the inability to see a positive future. I don't know about you, but if I lost my ability to imagine my future I think I would feel depressed.

Let me ask you a question. Imagine that after you finished reading this book, you went to bed and fell into a deep comfortable sleep. And just as you fell asleep, something magical happened. You woke up in the morning and the problem or negative behaviour you had yesterday had just disappeared. What would be the first thing you would notice?

After you have answered this question, wonder about the following.

- What else do you notice about yourself?
- How do you feel?
- Imagine looking at yourself standing in front of you. In what way do you look different?
- What does your partner, best friend or (whoever) notice about you?
- What do you notice about them?

See yourself at a week, two weeks and one month in the future. And ask the above questions again. Now take yourself three months into the future. How are things different?

Keep working on this magic question, building upon it each day; add more and more details to it as you go along. I use this process with many of my clients, and we usually achieve excellent results. See if you can stretch this magic question through to next year. This magic question technique can help you build a compelling future. This can also be helpful when working on relieving depression because it helps us to visualise a new positive future.

CHAPTER 8

THE MAGIC POWER OF AWARENESS

Awareness is the first step towards change.
MARCUS D'SILVA

Before we can expect lasting change, we have to become aware of ourselves. The more aware we are of ourselves, the more we know ourselves – our minds, our wants and our desires. It takes patience to learn about who we are. We may *think* we know who we are, but the truth is that we *only* think we know who we are. Only through being aware of our thoughts, feelings and behaviours can we discover the true essence of our selves.

THE PRESENT IS *NOW*

It truly is a gift to be able to live in the present. Perhaps that's why they call it the 'present'. When we experience the present without remembering the past or imagining the future, we are in a state of grace. We experience zero stress and anxiety, because in the present moment, there is no stress or, in actuality, distress. We are centred and calm; our bodies are relaxed. It is a wonderful place to be. The reality is that to live in the present moment all the time is impossible. It is natural for our brains to move from the present to the past and on to the future. If it were not, we wouldn't need goals in our lives, because we wouldn't be able to imagine them. We wouldn't see beyond today, which is an important part of creating our future. However, being able to experience the present can be a positive thing, because when we experience the present, we are aware and relaxed. Our creative juices start to flow, our blood pressure lowers, our heart rates slow down and tension is greatly reduced. So if you want to give yourself a gift, spend a little time in the present each day.

Exercise

Sit comfortably with your back straight. Put your hands on your thighs and your feet flat on the floor. Close your eyes and tune into your breathing. Just notice the natural rhythm of your breath. Notice the points where your breath begins and where your breath ends. Any thoughts that drift into your mind … just become aware of the thought and let it go, and gently bring your awareness back to your breathing. Your only concern is to be aware of your breathing. Any time you find yourself daydreaming or thinking about your work or personal issues, just gently bring your awareness back to your breath. You may notice your breathing naturally changes. That's fine – just be aware.

Exercise

Sit comfortably with your back straight. Put your hands on your thighs and your feet flat on the floor. Close your eyes and become aware of your breathing. As your mind begins to settle become aware of any sensations in your body. Tune into them, and become aware of any aches, pains, feelings … and become aware of thoughts without trying to judge them. Just observe them. As soon as the feeling or thought disappears, allow your awareness to move to another feeling, thought or sensation. Any time you find yourself losing focus, just gently bring your awareness back to your breathing. Start off by practising these meditations for 10 to 15 minutes a day.

Exercise

As you learn to expand your awareness of thoughts, feelings and sensations, you will discover that you can use this process to work on problems and challenges.

Sit comfortably with your hands relaxed on your thighs and your feet on the floor. Close your eyes and focus on a problem. Start to sense what you are feeling inside. Notice what images, words or thoughts come with this feeling …

As you continue to focus on the problem, allow yourself to be open to any new insights about what needs to done to help you further resolve this problem.

If you don't receive any insights to your problem try the following. Find an image or a thought that changes the unpleasant sensation (a word, picture or symbol, for example) to something more positive. Take your time. When you have discovered the thought or image, use it in the future to replace the old feelings.

If you find this difficult, and you don't succeed the first time, leave it and come back to it later.

TAKE A POWER BREAK

There are many books that tell us how to visualise things in our minds and construct affirmations as a way of programming our minds to get results. Yes, all of this works

– very well, if done correctly. What is not so clear is the best time to do this inner work. Recent research has shown that each of us enters a natural down time many times throughout the day.

It is a special time of the day when our mind/body is letting us know we need to take a break – perhaps a period of peaceful meditation, or a time to lie down and relax. This may also be the perfect time for creating inner changes, working on negative habits and behaviours, or discovering a solution to a problem.

In his ground-breaking book, *The Twenty-Minute Break*, Doctor Ernest Rossi shares the secrets of the ultradian rhythms. These are mind/body signals that we experience every 90 to 120 minutes, and they are a natural time to take a rest and allow ourselves the opportunity to heal and rejuvenate. They are a message from nature, letting us know we have an opportunity to de-stress or do some inner problem-solving. Maybe we want to make an important decision or tune into our natural creativity. Or maybe we are looking to get to work on an important health issue. The next time you find yourself gazing out of a window during the middle of your work day, or losing concentration, you are receiving a signal that it's time to take a power break.

The ultradian rhythm was discovered through the work of Dr Milton Erickson, one of the greatest hypnotherapists of our time. After careful observation, he found approximately 90 minutes into the therapy session, his clients would naturally slip into a trance state. When therapy was carried out at this time, amazing things happened – and the client improved immeasurably.

Thanks to Dr Rossi's discoveries, I personally have had incredible results with clients by using the ultradian rhythms. Whenever the clients I work with practise 'taking a break' every 90 to 120 minutes, wonderful things occur, behaviours change, and people become free from habits and addictions. They literally see their lives change.

How long?
Most people like us live busy, hectic lives. Time is necessarily limited, for each of us only gets 24 hours every day to do what we have to do. The optimum length of time for a power break is 15 to 20 minutes. I usually suggest to my clients that they aim to take a 15- to 20-minute break, twice a day. You may feel it is easier to take several mini-breaks each day – say five or six minutes, three or four times a day.

How to take a power break
If you are sitting at a desk all day, you could spend your power break going for a relaxing walk or doing a few stretches. If you are busy rushing around, sit down and relax. You could also find a quiet corner and do absolutely nothing. Let your mind wander, to lead you within. We live in an age of overwhelming, mass communication and information. If ever we needed regular power breaks, now is that time. And as more and more people start to work at home, it will become easier and easier to take advantage of our mind/body signals.

The benefits of power breaks are limitless, and include:

- Less tension and stress
- Enhanced creativity
- Better decision-making
- Increased energy levels

- Enhanced spirituality
- Superior motivation
- Improved overall health.

Better still, once you develop the ability to recognise your mind/body signals you will find you can really begin to take control of your life.

When to take a power break

Imagine you are sitting at your computer. You have been working hard for the last two hours or so. All of a sudden you find you lose concentration – maybe you start to gaze into space. You feel yourself starting to trance out. Something is telling you to take a rest; you go into your bedroom and lie down, close your eyes and relax for 15 to 20 minutes. When you open your eyes, you feel refreshed and alert.

Even if your work situation makes it difficult for you to rest for too long, shorter power breaks can still be beneficial to your health and wellbeing. You may also be surprised to find you begin to experience an increased level of performance in your work as a result.

Exercise

The next time you feel the need to take a break, try this.

Sit down and rest your hands comfortably on your thighs, with your feet flat on the floor. Close your eyes and relax. And let nature do its work. When a part of you knows it's time to come back to full awareness, just allow yourself to become fully aware and wide awake.

You will find that this process happens naturally, if you are entering a natural down time. You can literally close your eyes and do nothing. Just close your eyes and wonder to yourself what you may experience as you continue to relax deeply.

The more you can be aware of these natural rest cycles, and the more you use them, the more in tune with your inner nature you will become.

Exercise

When you feel the need to take a rest, sit down and bring your awareness into your body and allow yourself to relax. As your comfort deepens, focus on a goal, or a habit you want to change. Use self-talk to help you make that change. Utilise the principles of hypnotic language discussed on page 34.

You might choose to practise mental rehearsal, or work on your self-image. Be as creative as you choose.

CHAPTER 9

MEMORY: IT'S ONLY YOUR STORY

I have spent most of my life worrying about things that never happened.
MARK TWAIN

Every day of our lives we tell and listen to stories. Some are other people's stories, but many are our own. We run stories about past problems, future problems and even problems that don't exist. I'm not suggesting that we ignore these stories and memories; in some cases, they may be partly and even completely true recollections of events; however, in most cases they are our *perception* of events.

Let me explain. Our memories are not completely accurate. If you and I were to go for a walk around an art gallery for a day, we would both have a different story to tell about the experience. Memory is a process more than an event. If you and I were identical as people, it's likely our stories would be the same. But because we are all completely different we process information in different ways, and 'save it' on our internal hard drives in completely different formats. So what we remember may not actually be a true reflection of what actually occurred; it can be altered by the way we are feeling at the time, the emotions it evoked, the people we were with, and our own individual processing skills.

CHANGE YOUR STORY AND CHANGE YOUR LIFE

If our memories will never be 100 percent accurate, what does this mean in relation to our problems? It simply means that we often distort the perception of those problems. We have a story, and by story I mean a memory or series of memories or recollections that build up a picture of ourselves, which effectively becomes 'our story'. So one man's story might be that he can't lose weight; another woman's story is that she has no confidence. What do you think your story is?

What does this have to do with hypnosis? Everything! Anything that happens in our imagination can be termed hypnotic. The reality is that our perceived problems are a result of the way we use our imaginations, the way we process information, and the way we communicate with ourselves. The good news is that we can also use our minds to create solutions.

We can create stories that move us towards positive change. We can tell ourselves stories of how successful we are. We can design stories that make us happier and healthier. It's up to you. What do you want? You may have been telling yourself how shy you are, or how you are unworthy of good things. Our stories are powerful; salespeople and master persuaders use stories all the time to influence us. If it helps us to have a better life, that's a good thing. Remember the most famous book in history, the *Bible*, is a really just a bunch of stories, yet it has had a massive impact on millions of people around the world.

So if the stories people tell us are that powerful, imagine how powerful they are when we tell them to ourselves! We create different types of stories, of course: blaming stories, not-taking-responsibility stories, it's-impossible stories, and stories about how other people's interests, thoughts and feelings are wrong. Our stories are formed by our own beliefs, attitudes and expectations, which is why they are unique to us. It's also why they are, to us, true, even if they are not the same as anyone else's. We believe our stories because they form our reality.

But it's important to remember that you are the author and the editor of your stories. When you put your mental pencil to work, remember that old scripts can be rewritten. This doesn't mean that you are 'lying' or rewriting the past; instead it is looking at things through fresh eyes and getting something new and positive from the experience.

How can you rewrite your own personal scripts? Your present scripts will be influenced by what has happened in the past, but as you become aware of this, you can write new, positive scripts that move you into a more compelling future. You can also edit the old ones that have had such an impact on your life. For example, do you have an 'I'm shy' story, based on one or more experiences you've had in the past? Go back to those experiences and look at them again. Were you *really* shy, or were you the victim of circumstances? Did your lack of confidence, or something you were wearing, or doing make you feel unworthy or uninvolved? With the benefit of hindsight put a different spin on the story. For example, you had a difficult experience but you held your own, or you now realise you stood out because you weren't afraid to be different. Find the positive and see how that filters through to your current stories.

Exercise

Close your eyes and relax, as you bring your awareness into your body, your breathing, your thoughts. Begin to focus on a current problem. Tune into how your thoughts, words and images are creating your story. Become aware of how you are focusing on that problem. Notice the language that goes with this problem.

Maybe you are talking about how you will never be able to lose weight or speak in front of a large group. Become aware of the words you are using. You are almost certainly using words and statements that are focusing on the problem. When you have an awareness of the story you have created, start to change the way you view the story.

Maybe it was influenced by the views or actions of your parents or school teachers. I remember being given some extremely negative messages from some of my teachers, such as: 'You won't get a job because you are stupid.' And, yes, I did create a story from that experience, and it took me some years before I realised it was only me who had the power to change it.

Now slowly start to change the story: build a story of how you can be more confident or become free from cigarette smoking. Imagine seeing, feeling and hearing yourself as a non-smoker, or an immensely confident negotiator. Start to create images of these important changes. Talk to yourself about how you can feel, act and sound confident. Begin to focus on how and what you want to become.

CHAPTER 10

GOING FOR IT IN LIFE

If you want to do something, do it!
PLAUTUS

Somebody once asked the question: *What would you do in life, if you knew you couldn't fail?*

Think about it, because the answer could change your life. In fact, the right answer along with the right actions *will* change your life! This could be something as simple as starting a new exercise programme or something as big as starting a new business. What would you do? Answer this question and you have a challenge in front of you. That challenge is to go for it. It has been found that when we set ourselves a lofty goal we tend to perform to our best. The biggest reason why many people don't reach their goals is because they don't put enough juice into them. They are wishy-washy; they don't stir the emotions to the point that action follows. How is this? Why don't we invest more of our time in worthwhile goals? The main reasons are, as we explored earlier, fears – fear of success, of losing face, of failure, or criticism, or anything else that frightens you, even on an unconscious level.

There are a few things that *are* necessary for your goals to become a reality, and these include:

- *Desire*: You have to *want* to achieve your goal; it has to excite you.

- *Self-esteem*: Do you feel you are worthy of achieving this goal? Are you confident in your abilities to get the job done?
- *Energy*: You need energy to reach worthwhile goals. Are you putting the right fuel into your body? Are you getting enough sleep?
- *Attitude*: This is important; a positive mental attitude is basic to achieving worthwhile goals.

If you can honestly say 'yes' to all the above, then you have the tools you need to go for your goals. Remember the best goals are the ones that challenge you, because they produce personal growth – and that, my friend, is the secret to a wonderful life.

THE BEST WAY TO PREDICT YOUR FUTURE IS TO MAKE IT HAPPEN

Fortune-telling is big business. Millions of people flock to see Tarot card readers, mediums and astrologers for answers to their problems. It can be comforting to be told you are going to meet the person of your dreams within the next six months, or that there is a large sum of money coming from a long-lost relation. It's nice to know what the fates have in store for us.

But wait a minute. What this really tells us is that we have no control over our lives and that our future is pre-determined. Most people would rather believe that their destiny is in someone else's hands than to take responsibility for their own lives. This is a serious error, because if you don't make your own choices in life someone else will make them for you. Imagine a total stranger mapping out your life for you. Scary, isn't it? Yet this is what millions of people do. As we have seen the mind is very suggestible, especially when our emotions are involved. When a psychic tells you a story of how your life is going to change, he or she influences you by appealing to your emotions. You then visualise it, and it becomes a self-fulfilling prophecy.

The real secret to happiness and success is to create it yourself. No-one is coming to your rescue. Only you have the power to predict your future. And the good news is that when you decide to take responsibility, you are exercising your personal power. You are no longer relying on other people to tell you what you need to do, because you have all the answers inside yourself. When we take the time to listen to our inner selves, we learn more about ourselves; when we choose to go within we are choosing to trust our own inner adviser and that leads to real growth and change.

As we have seen, we are goal-directed beings. We need goals, and when we learn how to set goals we learn how to predict our own futures. Without goals we leave our lives to chance, and that's the truth.

THE POWER OF SMART GOALS

What are smart goals? They are goals that ensure your success. For goals to be effective they have to be:

- *Specific*: Your goal needs to be specific. You can't be thinking '*Maybe* I want this' or 'Let's see how it goes'. You have to be able to define your goals. You have to think to yourself 'This is what I want to achieve' and mean it.

- *Measurable*: Can your goal be measured? It needs to be. Do you know when you are getting closer to your goal? For example, if you want to slim down to a 34-inch waist or drop a dress size, you can see the changes happening before you. If you want to save a certain amount of money, you can check your bank account.
- *Achievable*: Seriously, ask yourself this question: 'Can I achieve this goal?' Winning a million on the lottery would be great, but it is not an achievable goal; giving up smoking within two weeks is.
- *Realistic*: Can you realistically achieve this goal? It is realistic to become more confident in your work; it is not realistic to be confident in everything you do for the rest of your life.
- *Time-orientated*: As you move toward your goal, make sure you have a time frame. If you don't, you'll be left with another 'New Year's Resolution' – yes, the kind that lasts no longer than the end of January. Remember, tomorrow never comes.

If you can say 'yes' to the above, you are on the road to success.

Put some juice in your goals
Remember that life is about *passion*. The more passionate you are about your goals, the better the outcome. If your goals don't excite you, find ones that do! When your goals have juice, you have a burst of energy. When this happens, nothing on earth can stop you from achieving them.

Each and every one of us wants to achieve something in life. If this is not true for you, then you had better start thinking about what it is you *do* want. I believe that one of the reasons people depress themselves is because they have no real aims or goals in life. We all need to have a future in front of us – if we don't we lose our purpose in life. One thing that people with depression have in common is that they find it difficult to imagine the future. This shows in their choice of language. They might say, for example, that 'The future looks hazy' or 'The future looks dim' ... or bleak. This is the opposite of someone who is motivated to achieve their goals, and for whom the future looks 'bright'.

Seeing is believing

We have to be able to see the end result. We have to be able to picture or imagine ourselves having reached our goal. As we discussed earlier, everything you have in your life now started as an image in your mind – a tiny piece of energy that eventually manifested itself into reality. The truth is that if you don't programme your own mind, someone else will! You can choose to control your own destiny or leave it to someone else. Too many people spend their lives complaining about how nothing good ever happens to them. Here's the reality: if you don't have any life goals (either written down on paper or fixed firmly in your mind), nothing good *will* happen. Why? Because that's the way life works. Your happiness, success, and even your health, begins inside your own mind.

HOW TO PROGRAMME YOUR GOALS

First, choose something you want to achieve. Ask yourself if it is what you truly desire. You will only achieve your goals if they have juice! Wishy-washy goals won't get you anywhere. Make a decision to aim high. This could be a financial, sporting, or even a career goal. You may even want to lose 30 pounds of excess weight. Set your goal as high as you wish and, as long as it is achievable, you will get there.

Exercise

Close your eyes and relax. Make an image of the goal you would like to reach. See yourself looking proud and victorious. Make the image big and bright. Step into the image and sense the feelings of achievement you experience, having reached your goal.

Imagine all of your friends and family, your partner and anyone who is supportive of you, standing around you cheering and celebrating your success! Maybe you can imagine them patting you on the back, telling you how well you have done.

Do this exercise once at the beginning of each day for 5 to 10 minutes. It will help keep your mind focused on your goal.

PART II

SELF-HYPNOSIS IN EVERYDAY LIFE

CHAPTER 11
STRESS: IT ALL DEPENDS
UPON HOW YOU LOOK AT IT

Skill to do comes of doing.
RALPH WALDO EMERSON

Stress is part of life. In fact it is a necessary part of life because we all need some stress to get things done. The adrenaline produced by the stress response gets us up and going, and hones our fighting instinct – an instinct that can be applied to virtually any area of our life to keep us sharp. Problems begin when stress exceeds our 'stress threshold', and we become distressed.

In the beginning, man faced many different kinds of threats. He may have been faced with the threat of death by a wild animal or another hunter, or even a natural disaster. In this situation man had a choice – fight or flee. When the decision was made the distress evaporated. It didn't matter what choice he made – to stay and fight, or to flee the scene. Both actions utilised the adrenaline produced by his body, so he was able to physically de-stress, and because he had made a decision, his mental stress was alleviated. This is called the 'fight or flight' response and it still works the same way today.

Fighting or fleeing?
When you feel that you are under threat (real or imagined)

a part of your brain (the hypothalamus) sends a message to your body to release hormones – in particular epinephrine, otherwise known as adrenaline. This tells your body that trouble is ahead and it must be prepared. Your muscles tense up, your heart rate accelerates and your blood pressure increases. Now you have to act – either fight or flee. If we are unable to fight *or* flee we begin to experience distress, and this is unhealthy both physically and mentally.

In these modern times we face different kinds of stress, such as financial problems, traffic jams, and keeping up with the pace of life in this exciting new 24/7 age of information. Unfortunately, the body hasn't adapted to the new types of stress and still pumps out hormones such as adrenaline. But because we normally have nowhere to run, and nothing to fight, that adrenaline isn't dispersed, and it begins to cause a whole host of problems in our bodies. More importantly, perhaps, we don't have a simple decision to make (i.e. fight or flee), which would ease the emotional and mental distress.

There are a couple of obvious solutions – getting out and doing a little exercise to get the adrenaline out of our systems is one good bet. But this doesn't do much for our self-awareness. The other solution is to stop and make some decisions. Ease your mental stress by relaxing your mind.

The other important thing to do is to deal with our perception of stress. This has to do with our stress threshold. We all know people who appear to thrive on stress, and can handle more than their weight of the stuff. Others crumble at the first sign of problems. Is this a physical thing? No, the truth is that people perceive stress differently, and it is this perception that sets their stress threshold. So the guy who can handle anything probably can handle anything because he doesn't perceive most things to be a problem. They don't stress him. The crumblers probably feel every niggling indication that a problem might be nigh, and fall into stress mode as a matter of course.

So, when managing our stress levels, the first thing we need to do is to learn how to relax. The second thing we need to do is to look at stress in a different way. As they say in America, 'Don't sweat the small stuff'. It may sound trite, but it's good advice. Let things wash over you. Actively choose to ignore things that would normally rile you. Choose a different approach to life. Make this one of the first changes you make. If things that once stressed you to the rafters no longer have the power to affect you, you've raised your stress threshold, and you are not distressed. Perception is reality.

Stop being a plate-spinner

Most us feel that we don't have enough time. We are constantly planning, scheming and thinking, and then scrabbling around to try to achieve everything we set out to do. This is because we are naturally goal-directed beings. Goals are important, and most of us like to keep busy and working towards them. However, it is just as important to take 20 minutes, once or twice each day, to sit and do nothing – a time for emptying our minds and recharging our batteries. I am reminded of an ancient story that explains this point:

> *Long ago, God sent an angel to earth with an offer of eternal life for just one moment of time on earth. Sadly, the angel returned without any offers, no-one had a moment of time*

*because everyone on earth had one foot in the past and one
foot in the future. No-one had anytime to spare for the
present.*

As a child, back in the 1970s, I remember watching an
entertainer spinning plates on top of what looked like
broom handles. He would run around the stage doing his
best to keep those plates spinning. If he were to lose control
of those plates, his act would be ruined. Yet this just what
many people do everyday of their lives – and they wonder
why they feel stressed!

When we try to do too many things at once we create
mental stress. The best advice I have ever heard is this: *The
best way to achieve a lot is to do one thing at a time.* It's true that
sometimes we may have many different things going on in
our lives, but the fact is that when we try to do too much we
suffer. We are more productive, satisfied and relaxed when
we do things one at a time.

Many gurus talk about the importance of time
management, but the truth is this: *You can't manage time, you
can only manage yourself.* None of us has the power to
manage time, but when we learn how to manage ourselves,
we will have the ability to take on more projects and
maintain a healthy state of mind. Time management is self-
management.

Relax your mind first

The ability to relax can lead to life changes. I am not talking
about watching TV or lying on the sofa. I am talking about
deep mental and physical relaxation. When we really learn
to relax and let go of tension we experience many changes
within. We are able to temporarily suspend our present

beliefs and attitudes. We are able to get in tune with our inner nature and start to work on changing habits and behaviours.

Trance: the key to relaxation

Trance is a natural part of our life experience, and the most natural and effective way of experiencing it in order to relax is through your breath. There is no need to learn special breathing techniques; all you need to do is focus on points of the breath. When we spend time focusing on where the breath begins and where the breath ends we build a bridge from our conscious mind to our subconscious mind. The wonderful thing about self-hypnosis or trance is that we can use it for a few minutes, or up to an hour, if we please. We can access it through words or through our awareness – through our breathing, for example, through the sounds around us, or our feelings. Try the following exercise to experience it for yourself.

Exercise

Sit comfortably with your hands resting on your thighs and your feet flat on the floor. Close your eyes and tune into your breathing.

As you begin to become aware of your breathing, allow your body to become more and more comfortable. As you *really* begin to tune into your breathing, become aware of what you hear. Maybe the traffic outside or perhaps the ticking of the clock. Whatever you notice yourself noticing, just be aware of it. Now become aware of the sensations in your hands.

Wonder about those hands – perhaps one hand is feeling heavier or lighter than the other. Is one hand warmer or cooler than the other? Just wonder about those possibilities.

Does it feel as though one hand wants to float up, as if there is a gas helium balloon tied to your wrist with a piece of string? And as you continue to notice the changes in one, or perhaps both of those hands, you may find you are becoming more and more comfortable with each breath you take.

And you can wonder ... Will your arms relax before or after your legs? Is your left foot more or less relaxed than your right? That's right ... allow yourself to relax more deeply now. As you allow yourself let go even more ... that's right ... really let go.

Now gently bring your awareness back to your breath. Begin to notice where your breath begins and where your breath ends. Maybe you can become aware of the middle of each breath. Simply observe your breathing. Suggest to yourself that you are becoming more and more relaxed, with each breath you take ...

... as you allow your mind to drift to pleasant scenes in your imagination ...

- A beautiful, white sandy beach
- A peaceful meadow
- Or maybe some other place that's special for you

As you find yourself there, see what you see, hear what you hear and feel what you feel. Just enjoy the feelings of comfort spreading deeply throughout your body.

In your own time allow yourself to drift back to full awareness, feeling relaxed and refreshed.

Another trance experience

Perhaps the best way to enter a relaxed hypnotic state is by using your ongoing experience. By using this method, nothing can become a distraction because, whatever you hear, feel or see helps you to experience deep relaxation.

Exercise

Sit comfortably with your hands resting on your thighs and your feet on the floor. Bring your awareness to your hands. Notice what you are experiencing in those hands. Maybe one hand feels lighter or heavier than the other. Is one hand more or less relaxed than the other?

Gently bring your awareness to your breathing. Notice where each breath begins and where it ends. Just tune into your breathing. Think of your breath as a natural rhythm of life, like the ocean waves, rolling onto the beach with each inward breath, and rolling out with each outward breath.

Imagine the ocean waves rolling into the shore as you breathe in, and the waves rolling out, as you breathe out. Maybe you can hear some traffic sounds? If so, imagine those sounds becoming the noise of the sea. Perhaps you can hear other sounds that can be creatively transformed into your experience: the clock ticking may become the beating of your heart; a plane in the sky can fly into the distance, as you imagine any worries or concerns flying away. Maybe you hear voices outside? Imagine those voices as your inner voices, faraway – giving you some time for yourself. Use your own ongoing experience and creativity to create your own trance.

Exercise

This is known as the 'enter-exit' technique, and can create a profound trance experience.

Sit or lie down. Allow yourself to be comfortable. Become aware of your breathing, tune into the natural rhythm of your breath, sense the natural rise and fall of your chest

As you breathe in, focus on the tension, anxiety or concern that is bothering you. Exaggerate it, increase the tension, anxiety or concern, really feel it. Then, as you breathe out, imagine it melting away. Say to yourself as you breathe out, *letting go*, and let it go.

Now tense the whole of your body tightly, from your feet up to the top of your head. Hold it. As you feel the tension increasing, let it go – and imagine your body melting as you say to yourself, *letting go,* and then let it go.

Repeat this process several times, and notice how more relaxed you become.

You can also break this process down into smaller pieces by slowly working through your body, tensing and relaxing each body part: your feet, your legs, your arms and chest. As you bring your awareness to each body part, make sure you tense it: clench your fist, squeeze together your toes, or tighten your abdomen. Then hold for a few seconds before letting them go.

Exercise
Sit or lie down, close your eyes and gently bring your awareness into your body. Imagine the muscles in your body slowly relaxing from the top of your head, all the way down to the tips of your toes. Now let yourself float back to a time in the past when you felt calm and relaxed, a time when you were free of tension.

As you drift back to that time, see what you saw, hear what you heard, and feel what you felt. Imagine the comfortable feelings spreading through your body. Allow the feeling to deepen. Sense the good feelings inside …

After a few minutes, drift back to full awareness, bringing those good feelings with you.

Read through the above exercises several times and then sit comfortably and practise them. You don't have to memorise them word for word; feel free to be as creative as you please. Do, however, remember to follow the rules of hypnotic self-talk (see page 34). The words you choose will make the exercises more effective and powerful. If you prefer, you can read out these scripts into a recording device and play them back to yourself. Remember to speak in a slow relaxed tone of voice, and replace the word you with the word I, e.g. I am relaxing deeply…

CHAPTER 12

BOOST YOUR SELF-ESTEEM AND CREATE UNSHAKEABLE SELF-CONFIDENCE

He who has lost confidence can lose nothing more.
BOISTE

When we talk about self-esteem, we are talking about our self-worth – our right to be here, and our divine right to walk this earth. Without an abundance of self-esteem we are going to have a different experience in life to someone who has *chosen* high self-esteem. In his wonderful book, *The Six Pillars of Self-Esteem*, Nathaniel Brandon talks about the different components of the self-esteem concept, which include self-efficacy and self-respect:

- *Self-efficacy* is your confidence in the ability to choose, understand, learn and make decisions, in the area of your interests and needs. It is the ability to trust your own mind.
- *Self-respect* is the assurance of your self-value, asserting your desires and needs. It involves feeling that happiness and harmony is what you deserve.

If you think about it, your self-esteem controls your levels of happiness, success, and even your health. If we want to progress in our careers or build a successful business, we need an abundance of self-esteem. If we want to have healthy, fulfilling relationships, we need healthy self-esteem. When we don't experience this state of being, we are not living as our true, authentic selves and, as a result, will not reach our full potential.

THE SELF-ACTUALISED PERSON

Out of the wisdom of American psychologist Abraham Maslow came the five levels of human needs. He theorised that when we achieve the highest of these needs, after working up the hierarchy, we become 'self-actualised'. This means that we become the person we were meant to be – the person we are capable of being. We are using our talents, skills and capabilities in our lives. We are living in line with our true inner nature. This also means we are being true to ourselves. We are calmer, we live with passion, and we become happier and healthier as a result. We also have a deeper understanding of ourselves as well as others, and there is expanded awareness and a feeling of wholeness.

In his original work, Maslow described the self-actualised person as having 'more efficient perception of reality and more comfortable relations with it'. In many ways that means that we have accepted who we are, and we can work with it, rather than against it.

Before we reach self-actualisation, there are four other levels of needs in the hierarchy. They are:

1. *Physical needs* for survival, such as food, water, clothing, shelter and sex.

2. *Security needs*: to be protected and looked after and to be kept safe.
3. *Love needs*: to be loved, which includes the need for social relationships and a sense of belonging.
4. *Esteem needs*: which relate to self-esteem, self-respect, and the need to achieve and accomplish. This also includes the need for confidence and self-worth.

The fifth need is self-actualisation: the need to become the person we should and can be.

A self -actualised human being
It's interesting to look at Maslow's work, because he is saying that we cannot be concerned about having high self-esteem if we haven't had our lower needs met. This would explain, for example, why a bankrupt businessperson may naturally lose self-esteem; he's lost everything he owned, and needs will become focused on the lower levels of the hierarchy, such as food and shelter. A person who has been divorced may be more concerned with needs of security. And so on.

The majority of people in Western society have their most basic needs met. There are, however, many people who need to feel more secure, and to be loved. There are even more people who need higher levels of self-esteem in their lives. When we achieve that higher self-esteem, we can work on becoming self-actualised.

POSITIVE SELFISHNESS

I was sitting on a plane recently, waiting for take-off. As the steward took us through the safety procedures I was reminded of the importance of positive selfishness. The steward told us that in the unlikely event that we needed to use the oxygen masks we had to make that sure we attended to ourselves first, before we helped others. This is a simple yet important example of positive selfishness.

The truth is that healthy selfishness is a positive thing. Let me explain. Each and every one of us has a responsibility to ourselves for making the best of ourselves. It is wrong to hold back on moving forward to achieve goals that we desire. We are creative beings; we are not here just to fulfil the needs of others. We have to put ourselves first before we are of any *use* to others.

Selfish, *yes*. Uncaring, *no*. I am not suggesting that you don't help others, and I am not suggesting you don't share and listen to others. What I am saying is that you have got to be true to yourself. If you want to take up a creative hobby, or get yourself a Masters degree – that's what you should do. You might have to work hard and burn the midnight oil, and you will have to pay a price. You may have to give up other things in your life in order to focus on yourself, but it is the right thing to do. For one thing, you will be more positive and fulfilled – which is a tangible quality that can be passed on to others. What's more, when we practise positive selfishness, we are putting ourselves in a better position to help others. It's difficult to help others when we can't even help ourselves. Most successful and happy people are selfish in a healthy way.

NEGATIVE SELFISHNESS

Becoming aware of the power of selfishness does not mean that we should take advantage of others or refuse to help them. This approach is the type of negative selfishness of which this world needs a lot less. All of us have an obligation and, in fact, an innate need to help and support others. All of us need help and support at different times of our lives, and what we give, we tend to get back. It is also a positive feature of the human condition that we are programmed to help others. But this is something entirely different from 'positive' selfishness.

To be happy and successful we have to learn positive selfishness. The opposite of this is to be selfless, which means abandoning our dreams and ambitions. It means becoming reactive to circumstances and people around us. When we do this, we become resentful, angry or even depressed; to give up these things is to give up our self-esteem. Remember, positive selfishness leads to higher self-esteem and that's a good thing.

SELF-ACCEPTANCE: YOUR KEY TO FREEDOM

Has your ego been tricking you? Are you rejecting or accepting yourself? One of the lost secrets of change is the ability to accept ourselves unconditionally. Most people don't. Yet every time we choose to reject ourselves we continue to move away from change. Most of us are programmed to believe that we should love others first, and put others before ourselves.

But it just can't work this way. We cannot truly make others happy if we are not happy ourselves. When we learn how to accept and love ourselves unconditionally, we can move forward and grow. We can be truly free from whatever it is that is preventing us from living happy, healthy and successful lives. Sometimes the ego (our sense of self) trips us up and sabotages our efforts. We tell ourselves we are not worthy, or we are stupid. But that's just our ego talking. It's not really us at all – not the real us that lies deep within. So, the key to lasting change lies within your ability to accept yourself and treat yourself with unconditional love.

It's worth noting too that self-acceptance and self-love creates a sense of tolerance and understanding of others; it makes us better people, able to understand the actions, motivations, beliefs and feelings of others, because we've had a glimpse of them within ourselves. When we accept ourselves we can accept others.

SIX WEEKS TO HIGHER SELF-ESTEEM

Whenever you are not accepting yourself you are effectively rejecting yourself. This concept can, and does, create resistance with some people. Why? Because it seems that accepting something in our lives makes it unchangeable. However, the opposite is true. The reality is that when we choose to accept something about ourselves, we have a much better chance of changing it. Now, to accept we have to experience. It's not enough to just say, 'I accept I am 30 pounds overweight'; we have to *experience* it first. Obviously we have experienced the physical sensation of carrying around 30 extra pounds; however, we need to experience – get inside – the feelings that go with being overweight at a more deeper level of awareness. When we truly begin to accept ourselves, we can change. Remember this is a positive act, not a negative one. If we are not accepting we are rejecting. So when you discover the power of self-acceptance you will find yourself more motivated to change the things that are within your power to change. The following exercises will help you to build more self-esteem in your life.

Exercise

The purpose of this exercise is to put you more at ease and in harmony with yourself. It will also increase your motivation to make changes. Remember that self-acceptance is about becoming aware of the reality of how it really is. When we find ourselves accepting ourselves unconditionally, then we can move towards lasting change. You may find the following exercise uncomfortable to begin with, and that's OK. Many of my clients tell me that after two to three weeks of doing this exercise they begin to feel more at ease with themselves and, of course, more accepting.

Stand in front of a full-length mirror, naked or in your underwear. Look closely at yourself and notice how you feel inside. Tune into the feelings. As you do this, start to look closely at yourself. Look at the features on your face. You will find many things you don't like about yourself, and some things you do. As you slowly move down your body, just accept what you see. Say to yourself, *I choose to accept myself fully, completely and unconditionally.*

Repeat this several times to yourself. Continue the exercise for two minutes, once every morning and once every evening. You may be surprised at the change in yourself over the coming weeks.

Exercise

Imagine how differently you would feel if you loved yourself as much as the people closest to you love you. For some people this would be profound. I call this exercise 'the look of love'.

Close your eyes and allow yourself to relax. Imagine the person who most loves you standing in front of you. Picture the person in as much detail as you can. Make the image big and bright. Now imagine floating into this person, and seeing, feeling and hearing from their body …

Now look back at yourself, sensing the love and admiration they have for you. Now slowly float back into your own body, only as fast as you bring those feelings of love and admiration back into yourself.

Affirmations for self-esteem

Combine the following affirmations daily, with the exercises above.

- *I choose to bring more awareness into my life …*
- *I choose to bring more awareness to my relationships …*
- *I choose to bring more awareness to my work …*
- *I choose to be of high value to myself …*
- *I choose to honour my wants and needs …*
- *I choose to be lovable …*
- *I choose to trust my own mind …*
- *I choose happiness, because I am worthy of it …*
- *I choose to deal with life's challenges …*
- *I choose to express myself …*
- *I choose to be responsible for myself …*
- *I choose to be responsible for my life goals …*
- *I choose to assert myself …*
- *I choose to express my thoughts …*
- *I choose to be honest with myself and others …*
- *I choose to follow my dreams …*
- *I choose to be myself …*

SELF-CONFIDENCE

Confidence is crucial to our happiness and success in life because without it we cannot achieve anything worthwhile. We are mentally paralysed without the ability to be confident. We can't be our best because we block off our potential. When we project low levels of confidence we are not our true selves. It's impossible for us to be authentic. People pick up on this and, as a result, do not have as much trust or faith in us. After all, if we aren't confident about ourselves, why should anyone else be? If you are in the business of selling (and who isn't; see page 123) a product or service, your livelihood depends on communicating self-confidence.

Most people who believe they have no self-confidence do not see themselves as being confident. They have a poor self-image, and they do not feel worthy of sharing ideas or asserting themselves. They think along the lines of, 'Who am I to teach these people?' and 'Who do I think I am?'

If you hold the belief that you have no confidence, the truth is that you don't. Nothing we do in life is done well without confidence. You can be the very best at something but without confidence you won't succeed. When we feel confident in our ability to achieve something we are able to communicate enthusiasm, and that's amazingly powerful. When we are enthusiastic we have the power to persuade and influence others, which is important in many areas of life, including our careers and our relationships.

Exercise

There are some good ways to programme your mind for confidence. Find a quiet space and give this a try.

Sit comfortably and allow yourself to relax. Tune into your breathing, as you notice yourself noticing where your breath begins and where your breath ends. And as you continue to relax, tune into the most comfortable part of your body. That's right, really relax.

Now, imagine watching yourself acting as you want to become. See yourself glowing with confidence – hear the confident sound of your voice. Notice the feelings of being relaxed and in control. Run the movie again and again in your mind.

Now ask yourself, *Do I like what I see*? If not, run the movie again and again until you *do* like what you see. If you think you could imagine yourself being more confident, imagine it happening. When you are happy with what you are seeing, feeling and hearing, step into the movie and experience the new behaviour from your own eyes.

Remember to see what you see, hear what you hear and feel what you feel. Run the new behaviour of being confident again and again, until it feels as through it happening now!

THE PHYSIOLOGY OF CONFIDENCE

This powerful technique evolved from the science of neuro-linguistic psychology. It demonstrates the power of using our physiology to create change at lightning speed. What's lightning speed? Well that all depends on what you are trying to change and how long your brain has been running the behaviour.

Its never fails to amaze me that people who have been overweight for most of their lives expect to change their weight and shape in a month! It is just plain unrealistic to expect that kind of change. On the other hand, if someone who has been confident most of his or her life seems to have temporarily lost that confidence, change can be rapid.

Exercise

Get yourself into a relaxed state. Take a few minutes to allow your nervous system to calm down. Now put yourself into that feeling of low confidence. Now, become aware of your physiology. Notice your posture,

Is it slumped? Are you looking downward? What is the tonality of your voice like?

When you do this it might be easier to look in a full-length mirror. Alternatively, you can do this exercise with a friend or someone you trust. Now put yourself into a confident, resourceful state. How would you be thinking? There was a time in your life when you acted confidently and you felt confident.

Let your mind go to that time in the past where you felt totally confident. You will start to notice your posture changing as you do this. Let your body move into this highly confident position. As you think back to this confident time in your life, see what you saw, hear what you heard and feel what you felt. You may be noticing that your posture has changed. Check the change in the mirror or get feedback from your partner.

When you are happy that you can put yourself into that state of total confidence, break the state. Stand up and move around. Now go back to your current state of low confidence. Again check with your partner or the mirror to see that you have the state back.

Now comes the exciting part!

As the negative state intensifies, quickly move your body

into the positive, confident state. As you connect with this new, resourceful state, shout a word (yes, *shout*) that matches this new confident state. Now go back to the negative state and repeat the process five times, each time *quickly* moving from the negative state! Shout the word as you get into the positive state.

Now try to get the negative state back. As you do this, you should find it harder to retrieve it. Repeat the exercise several more times until you find yourself going into the positive state automatically. If you find that you are still experiencing the negative state, go back and repeat the whole process.

Steps to the physiology of confidence

- *Step 1*. Go into the negative, low-confidence state. Take note of your posture and the sound of your self-talk, and notice where your eyes are looking – upwards, downwards, etc.
- *Step 2*. Now go into the positive, highly confident state and take note of your posture and the sound of your self-talk, and notice where your eyes are looking – upwards, downwards, etc.
- *Step 3*. Get back into the negative state, and *quickly* move into the positive state. When you reach your positive, confident state, shout out a word that matches this state: *amazing, confident, wonderful, focused.*
- *Step 4*. Repeat step 3, five times quickly, making sure you put as much emotion and energy into the movements and words as possible.
- *Step 5*. Repeat steps 3 and 4 until you can only experience the positive state.

- *Step 6.* Try to get the old negative state back; after 10 to 15 repetitions you will find it almost impossible to go into the negative state again.

To make these changes stick, practise steps 3 and 4 each day for five days.

CHAPTER 13

MAKING DECISIONS WITH SELF-HYPNOSIS

The difficulty of life is in the choice.
GEORGE MOORE

A part of me wants to go shopping, but a part of me wants to stay at home and relax. A part of me wants to buy that beautiful car, but a part of me doesn't. If this scenario sounds familiar to you, you aren't alone. Most of us at different times of our lives feel in conflict with ourselves about something – or everything! The sad part is some people spend months even years in this state of complete confusion.

We all have many different mind/body states. These are sometimes referred to as ego states or parts. When a part of you wants to do something and another part of you does not, there is a raging conflict going on inside. When we experience this battle within, we become stuck, unable to move forward – in a sense we become mentally crippled.

In many ways this is a positive thing. There is a positive intention to all sides of any argument, and the parts of you that support them. The person who has a part that wants to lose weight and a part that doesn't may be in conflict, but the part that doesn't want to lose the weight might be fearful that failure to achieve the desired weight could create disappointment and unhappiness.

The woman who suffered a broken heart may have a part of her that wants to keep herself overweight as a way of protecting her from looking attractive, meeting a mate and having the same hurtful experience again.

The man who goes broke through a bad business decision may have a part of him that does not want to go into another venture because he is fearful of it happening again and losing everything.

You may not be aware of any of these fears, or even understand in your conscious mind why a part of you seems so negative and contradictory. The reason is that this goes on at the unconscious level. Your unconscious mind does a wonderful job of protecting you, even though it may not always make complete logical sense.

Exercise

This is a good way to integrate your parts and make some changes.

Sit down comfortably, and close your eyes. Rest your hands comfortably on your thighs with your palms facing up. As you continue to relax, focus your mind on the part that of you that wants to do something – lose weight, stop smoking, or whatever. Imagine this part of you is resting in one of your hands. Feel the weight of that part. Imagine how it looks. It may even have a sound.

As you focus on that part, become aware of its positive intention – losing weight to be more healthy and attractive, or maybe quitting smoking to improve your fitness. There could be a part of you that wants to quit your job and part of you that doesn't, just focus on the part of you that wants to change.

As you continue to focus on this positive part, become

aware of all the positive intentions of the part. Now bring your awareness to your other hand. Focus all your awareness on the other part. Imagine the opposite part is resting in this hand. Become aware of the positive intentions of this part.

It may seem difficult at first – even impossible – but keep on searching for the positive intentions. If you smoke, maybe there is a part of you that wants to continue because it stops you from feeling bored. Or perhaps smoking gives you chance to take a break every hour or so.

Keep going backwards between the two parts, being aware internally of the positive intentions. Understand that each part of you has a positive intention; you just need to be aware of it. As you go back and forth between parts, you begin to notice that each part is doing a good job of running its behaviour for different reasons.

Continue to do this even if you are not sure whether the positive intentions are real.

Now imagine you have a superior part of you between your hands. It may be a higher or wiser part. Imagine that this superior part is helping you to integrate both of your parts together as one whole. When you have a sense of this superior part working to help you integrate, slowly bring your hands together as you imagine the parts becoming one whole. When you feel the integration is complete, bring both hands up to your chest, bringing the parts back into yourself.

After practising this technique several times you begin to experience more balance and control, helping you resolve your inner conflict.

CHAPTER 14

MAKING YOUR RELATIONSHIPS WORK

Friendship requires great communication.
SAINT FRANCIS DE SALES

One thing in life is certain: if our relationships aren't working, our lives can't be working well either. Enjoying good relationships with others is essential to our health and wellbeing. There can be a lot stress associated with being around people when harmony is out of balance. Unfortunately the world is full of unhealthy relationships that create misery and unhappiness.

Of greatest importance is the way we respond to the people we love and care for. If we don't communicate well with these people, life can be tough, really tough! Let's take marriage, for example. When two people meet and are attracted to each other, magic can happen. This is because our emotions become involved. We fall in love, we want to be with that person, and maybe we choose to marry that person. We make most of these decisions based on our emotions.

It is after a period of married life that we tend to think of the marriage in a more logical way. This is natural because, to a certain extent, we come out of our love trance (sometimes referred to as the honeymoon period), and use more logic in our relationship. When I refer to the term 'love trance', I am talking about a genuinely altered state of awareness – a highly emotional state that is called 'being in love'.

To a lesser extent, this is true of all relationships. We buy into the friendship, usually through our emotions. As time passes, we become more logical in the way we think about the other person. And as relationships develop, it's natural to experience conflict once in a while.

One area of communication that is extremely important in our closest relationships is how we respond to criticism. Are we always on the defensive or do we become angered by it? Do we feel we always have to be right? Maybe we don't listen enough? Perhaps we don't always choose the right words. If you think you are guilty of this behaviour then read on.

Exercise

This is an excellent technique for improving your relationships.

Sit comfortably with your hands on your thighs and your feet on the floor. Close your eyes and go inside. As you bring your awareness to your breathing, allow yourself to drift into a comfortable state of relaxation.

Now imagine yourself as number one (this will become clearer in a moment). Now imagine there is a number two you standing out in front of you. See the number two you talking with someone with whom you would like to communicate better. This might be your spouse or maybe a friend or a work colleague.

As you do this, imagine there is number three. That's you again, standing out in the distance, watching and observing number two you, communicating with this person. When you get a sense that you are watching the usual interaction you and this person may have, imagine the number two you now beginning to communicate in new, more creative ways, responding to criticism (or whatever) in new, healthier ways.

Anything that you don't like about your interaction, simply change. While all this is going on, number three you is over in the distance taking notes and observing all the new creative ways you have of responding. Continue with this for a while longer until you feel you are getting some new insights and are happy with your new responses.

Now imagine that the number two you is walking over and into the number three you. As this happens, be aware that number three you is taking in all the valuable new communication skills from the number two you.

Now imagine number three you is floating back into yourself, bringing back all the new learning. When you feel that numbers two and three you are fully integrated back into yourself, slowly come back to full awareness again, feeling relaxed and refreshed.

You might have to practise this a few times before you notice a change in your outer world, but most people quickly experience a positive improvement in their relationship.

CHAPTER 15

How to Quit Smoking and be Free from Tobacco

No matter how far you have gone on a wrong road, turn back.

TURKISH PROVERB

Over the years I have helped many people quit the cancer sticks. Those last two words may have been a little painful for some of you to read. But I make no apologies. There are millions of people out there who pay money to breathe in deadly, toxic chemicals.

The good news is that it is actually quite easy to stop. I know this because I have seen many of my clients quit in just 90 minutes! OK, some of them needed two sessions, and 20 percent of my clients chose to carry on smoking. But if you are one of the 80 percent who truly *desire* to succeed, then read on.

Imagine a scale of zero to 10, where 10 represents a huge desire to quit smoking, and zero is no desire at all. Where are you on that scale? If you are at seven or higher, then I like your chances of success. If you are lower than that, I suggest you go to the local cancer ward and see where you may be heading. The truth is we have to be responsible for our own lives. You have the right to make the choice to smoke, as long as you are aware of the dangers and the potential suffering.

Some people ask me if they can use self-hypnosis to quit smoking. The simple answer is *yes*. *Yes, if you have the desire.* In fact, many people stop smoking without any help at all. This is because they were able to link enough pain with the habit of smoking. When you can link enough pain to smoking tobacco you will quit too.

Some smokers feel that the damage has already been done – and that there is little point in giving up now, after a lifetime of puffing. But be assured, your amazing body can heal itself, and giving up is most definitely worth it. Let's look at the process:

- *After just 20 minutes*, your blood pressure begins to lower and your heart rate slows down.
- *After 8 hours*, the carbon-monoxide levels in your body return to normal.
- *After, or within, 3 months,* your lung function improves.
- *After 1 year*, your risk of heart disease is half that of someone who smokes.
- *After 5 years*, your risk of stroke is the same of someone who has never smoked.

Still with me? Follow the steps below to quit, once and for all.

- *Step 1.* Write down all the benefits of stopping smoking. Start with the strongest benefit. Keep writing until you get to the weakest benefit. This will help to start the process of change.
- *Step 2.* Write down how many cigarettes you smoke. Write down where and when you smoke them. Become aware of how you run your habit.

- *Step 3.* Make a date! Write on a piece of paper, 'I choose to become free from tobacco on (insert date)'. Read this statement out loud or in your mind 10 times each day, then wad the paper up in one of your hands and relax into a state of hypnosis (see page 83, 84 or 85). Imagine the words coming alive in your hand and spreading throughout your body as you relax deeply.
- *Step 4.* On the date you have committed to quit, sit down and do the following exercise.

Exercise

Relax into a comfortable hypnotic state. Imagine a crystal ball out in front of you. In the crystal ball, see yourself two years in the future, still as a smoker. Imagine how you feel, knowing you are still a smoker. See all the negatives of staying a smoker – perhaps your health is starting to suffer, or maybe you are coughing a bit more.

Now imagine another crystal ball five years in the future. See how your health has declined. Notice how awful you are feeling, having put another five years of poison into your body. Notice how you have aged. How much longer until you wreck your health completely? See another crystal ball 10 years into the future. What have the consequences been of staying a smoker? See, hear and feel your experience. Put as much pain into these images as you can. Pain, pain, pain!

Now imagine another crystal ball out in front of you. This time, see yourself one year into the future as a non-smoker. Imagine yourself feeling wonderfully proud of the fact that you chose good health and fitness. Notice how proud you feel. Notice how wonderful you are feeling. Feel yourself breathing easily. See yourself looking fit and healthy. Sense a feeling of relief, because you are free from that old habit.

Now see another crystal out in front of you. Picture yourself two years out into the future, still free from tobacco. Become more and more aware of the many benefits of being a non-smoker. Imagine yourself breathing in the fresh clear air. Sense an increase in energy. Picture yourself looking and feeling amazing. See yourself looking happy and healthy with the people you care about all around you. Float into those wonderful feelings and slowly float back now to the present, bringing all those positive feelings with you. *Positive feelings, positive feelings*!

- *Step 5*. For the next three weeks, go into hypnosis every day for 20 minutes. Picture yourself as a non-smoker. Make the image big and bright in your mind. Imagine yourself in many different situations where you used to smoke. Notice your hands are free of cigarettes. Picture yourself looking and feeling relaxed and confident. Make the image bigger and brighter, and step into the image.

Taking your change to the bank
Find a large jar, make a slot in the top of it, and seal the lid. Work out how much money you would have spent on cigarettes at the end of each week and put that amount into the jar. It is a powerfully motivating experience to watch the money mount up each week. Just imagine the amount you will save over a 12-month period. Make sure you use that money for something special, to reward yourself for a job well done.

CHAPTER 16

THE POWER OF
THINKING THIN

We fear the thing we want the most.
DR ROBERT ANTHONY

In my book, *Weight Loss–The Forgotten Secret*, I share a simple, four-step approach to lasting weight control. The process of losing weight is, of course, quite simple, but it's not always easy. Most people now realise that the only way to control weight is to eat less and move around more. *Heck!* How many times have you heard this? The problem is that we all want the magic bullet – a magical solution to make the process painless. But by now you know as well as I do that these magical solutions only lead to disappointment. However, clever marketers continue to get their way and we all continue to bite! The problem is that when we commit to making a change, perhaps even losing a little weight in the process, we tend to give up before we reach our goal. The weight piles back on, and our confidence and self-esteem take a shuddering blow.

It doesn't have to be that way. I am now going to give you three self-hypnosis techniques that will help you to turbo-charge your weight control. For a more in-depth understanding of using hypnosis to control your weight, read my book: *Weight Loss–The Forgotten Secret.*

FIRST THINGS FIRST

This may sound obvious, but it's a starting point that has to be undertaken. You know why.

- Start by walking *briskly* for 45 minutes every day. You can choose to walk for 15 minutes, three times a day. Or go for a long walk whenever it suits you. Do this for six days a week, and take a day off.
- Eat 25 percent less food every day. That means leaving a small portion of food on your plate, or using a smaller plate.

Exercise

We'll call this one 'hypnotic eating'.

Eat slowly. As the food enters your mouth, Feel the textures of the food as the food moves around in your mouth. Imagine the different colours and shapes. Roll the food from the tip of your tongue to the back of your tongue, and side to side – sensing and tasting each mouthful. Make your mealtimes a truly meditative experience.

Exercise

This exercise involves improving your self-image, a sure key to weight loss.

Relax into comfort any way you choose. Allow your body to really relax and let go. As your body continues to relax, picture yourself at your ideal weight. See yourself looking amazing at your ideal weight. Imagine yourself wearing the clothes your desire to wear. Feel the feelings of confidence as you step into the image. Now step out of the image and make it bigger and brighter – bring it closer. Think of a colour that matches what you see. Use that colour to put a frame around the image. You are now starting to think thin. Think of this image as your new inner blueprint. Whenever you think of yourself, imagine this image – as you exercise, while you walk, as you lay in bed at night, and whenever you have a few minutes of peace.

Exercise

I call this the 'aversion technique', and it is a powerful tool for weight loss.

Allow yourself to drift into a state of relaxed awareness. Progressively relax all the muscles in your body, starting from your head all the way down to your toes. As you allow yourself to drift deeper into soothing comfort, think about the most disgusting-tasting food you can think of. Find something that smells bad and probably tastes even worse. That's right, something really disgusting. It should have a taste and a smell that makes you feel slightly sick. When you feel you have a good representation of this in your mind, put the image to one side for a moment. Now start to picture a food, perhaps chocolate or some other food that you regularly feel compelled to eat – a food that sabotages your weight-loss efforts.

At this point it is important to *make sure you want to change your feelings towards this food*. If you enjoy eating this food and you want to keep it that way, *stop this exercise now*. If you want to lose your desire for this food, please continue.

Now bring back the disgusting image and slide it behind the sweet or fatty food you feel compelled to eat.

As you bring back your focus to the good image, make a

small hole in the middle of it. Now imagine that the bad image, along with the disgusting smell, is slowly flowing through, covering the good image. And as this is happening, try to feel compelled to eat the problem food (chocolate, or whatever). Repeat this exercise five times and, as the bad image flows through, try to get the urge to eat the food you used to enjoy. Now let the images go. And come back to full awareness.

Repeat this exercise until you associate the good image with the bad image. Be sure to bring the bad taste and the smell into the negative image.

Exercise

Give yourself some hypnotic suggestions.

Sit down and tune into your breathing. As you begin to relax, sense the comfort inside your body spreading. Imagine yourself on a beautiful beach or in a peaceful meadow – or some other special place that feels good to you. Wonder how deeply relaxed you can become, and wonder when you can enjoy smaller amounts of food. Wonder how you can discover new ways to exercise your body, and how you can enjoy this extra activity – because you want to lose weight. Imagine all the possibilities of change.

When you feel ready, drift back up to full awareness again.

THE BEST FOOD TO EAT

Although you can lose weight eating almost any type of food, it is sensible to give your body the right kind of fuel. After all you wouldn't put diesel into your car instead of unleaded – would you? Research has found that your body will burn fat more effectively if you follow a balanced, low-fat diet, with plenty of fresh fruits and vegetables; and research has also found that this type of approach will ensure that you do the best in the long term.

So, if you are serious about getting into shape and, at the same time, dramatically improving your health – read on.

Carbs are king
Carbohydrates are the foods that give us energy and should play a large part in our daily eating pattern. It is important though that we eat the right kinds.

Refined carbs
Refined carbs are the kind we need to keep to a minimum. They contain high levels of white sugar or flour, they have no nutritional value, and they should be considered treats.

Examples are:
- white bread
- cakes
- chocolate
- jams
- biscuits
- fizzy drinks
- processed, sweetened breakfast cereals.

Diets high in these foods will produce low energy levels, tiredness, irritability, and lack of motivation. In the long term they will lead to poor health.

Unrefined carbs
Including these carbs in your daily eating programme will make your weight-loss goals even easier, and they'll help

you to feel vital and alive. These types of carbs also play a big role in longevity, and in the long-term health of our mind and body.

Examples are:
- wholewheat pasta (or other unrefined grains, such as corn, quinoa or brown rice)
- potatoes
- wholegrain bread
- wholegrain cereals
- vegetables
- fresh fruit.

Proteins: The building blocks of life

An important ally to carbohydrates is protein. Protein plays a vital role in the function of all of our body cells, and helps to build and maintain muscle tissue. Contrary to popular belief we do not need large quantities of protein. We can meet our daily needs by eating one medium portion of the following foods. That's not to say that you can't have more of the foods that contain essential elements, such as fibre in pulses, or calcium in dairy produce, but be aware that one serving is enough to meet your protein needs:

- pulses
- fish
- chicken
- meat
- eggs
- cheese.

Good fats

We need fat for survival. It would be unhealthy and undesirable to have zero fat in our daily diet. It would also be very difficult, as there is fat in many foods. It is important, however, to choose the right type of fat to help our bodies to function at an optimum level. Using these oils in our diet will help us to live a more active, healthier and longer life.

Try to avoid saturated and hydrogenated fats whenever possible. There is plenty of evidence to suggest that these are harmful to our health. Instead choose oils such as:

- olive oil (extra virgin)
- flax oil
- sunflower oil.

The magic nutrient

As our bodies are comprised of over 75 percent water, it's not surprising that we need lots of it. Water is the number-one nutrient, and without it we can't survive. Only oxygen is more vital to our survival. Forgetting to drink water is like forgetting to breathe.

Water is vital to weight-loss success as it has no calories, cholesterol or fat. It encourages your kidneys to function properly which, in turn, help your liver to do one of its most important jobs – metabolising fat. It also keeps you feeling full. So make sure you include six to 10 glasses a day, as part of your weight control programme.

CHAPTER 17

BREAKING FREE FROM PAIN

Pain is never permanent.
SAINT TERESA OF AVILA

Like it or not, pain is a fact of life. All of us, at some point in our lives, have to endure some pain, whether it is emotional or physical. Both of these types of pain affect one another. When we experience physical pain, for example, we usually find that our emotional state is affected; similarly, when we suffer from emotional pain or distress we often experience physical symptoms. While emotional pain is as real and as potentially debilitating as physical pain, we will be dealing with the physical aspects of pain in this section.

Before you begin, I must stress that the pain-control techniques suggested in this book should only be employed *after* you've consulted a medical doctor. Pain is our body's way of telling us that something is wrong, and we do need to pay attention to the message. Complementary therapies, such as hypnosis, are ideal when pain becomes chronic – when it starts to take its toll, and nothing seems to touch it. I've personally found that hypnosis is extremely effective in the treatment of headaches and migraines.

Medication and other drug-related interventions can often supply some relief; however, there are normally undesirable side-effects as well, and most are habit-forming. That's one reason why so many people turn to hypnosis – that, and the fact that it works, of course!

When we work with pain, we sometimes have to use the pain itself as a way of inducing hypnosis. Trying to develop relaxation when in a state of discomfort can be an uphill struggle if the pain is severe. When suffering from any type of pain, most people tend to try and escape the sensations by trying to forget about it. This can be a good strategy, though people tend to bring their awareness back to the problem through the very act of 'trying' to forget it about it. As you'll recall, trying simply doesn't work. Have you ever tried to get to sleep, only to find that you become increasingly awake? The same goes with trying to forget about pain.

Exercise

This exercise focuses on the painful area.

Get as comfortable as you can. Tune into your discomfort. Ask yourself these questions, and give yourself plenty of time to receive an answer:

- In what area of my body do I feel my pain?
- Where does my discomfort start and where does it move to?
- Where does it end?
- Does the discomfort have a dull or sharp feeling?
- Is it warm or cold?
- Is the discomfort constant, or does it come and go?
- Is there a stabbing sensation or a throbbing sensation?

Spend some time and just wonder about these possibilities.

Now that you have explored these sensations and increased your awareness of the pain, the next thing to do is some 'symptom scaling'. On a scale of zero to 10, where 10 represents the most pain, and zero is the most comfortable, where on the scale are you? When you have discovered what level your pain is at, become aware of what imagery you are using to get that number.

For example, you might visualise a large dial with numbers going around it from zero to 10. Maybe you imagine a large lever or some type of control panel. When you envision the kind of imagery that matches your experience, imagine you are turning the pain up, slowly, all the way to number 10. As you do this, allow your pain to increase. Use your mind to increase your pain. I know you what you might be thinking: *I want less pain, not more!* But just continue to turn it up for a few moments.

When you are sure it is on a 10, slowly turn the dial down. As you do this, you may notice the discomfort beginning to reduce. Slowly turn it down to number three, and start to turn it up again. Repeat this process a few times, and after some practice you should be able to control the discomfort, bringing it all the way down to zero. It is important to remember that you must be able to *increase* the pain before you can work on reducing it.

Exercise

This is an excellent technique for pain that is localised. It allows you to 'displace' your pain.

Bring your awareness into your discomfort. Now, ask yourself: *What colour is the discomfort?* Normally, people say it's red or black, although it may be different for you. Now change the colour to a softer, calmer colour, like blue or green. Keep changing the colour until it doesn't seem to want to change anymore.

Now, what shape is it? If it's a disfigured blob, change it to a circle or a square – whatever shape first comes to mind. Keep changing the shape until it won't change anymore. Now shrink it, make it tiny and move it to a different location in space. Some people like to put it under their fingernail or keep it on the tip of their toe. By doing this, the pain is kept to a minimum.

You might need to practise this technique several times, before you notice a change.

Exercise

The easiest and most natural way of controlling your pain is to use distraction.

Think of something you do in life that absorbs you so much – something you do that seems to cause time just to fly by. For some it might be reading or writing; others find this happens when watching a good movie. Many people unconsciously distract themselves by becoming engrossed in an interesting task. You can use this strategy any time you find yourself experiencing pain.

THE COMMON HEADACHE

When we get a headache, it's normally a symptom of dehydration or tension. The best cure for a headache is to sit down; close your eyes and focus on your headache. Just become aware of the sensations you are feeling inside your head. Keep focusing on the feeling for eight minutes. Most people find after this time, the headache is gone. As the sensation vanishes, say to yourself: *The muscles in my head are relaxed. The muscles in my head are comfortably relaxed and I am feeling calm.*

Sometimes all that is needed is some simple relaxation. When the pain is of a low intensity, relaxing the body and mind can have a positive effect.

CHAPTER 18

THINK LIKE A SALES SUPERSTAR

---

*Before everything else, getting ready is the
secret of success.*
HENRY FORD

Salespeople could be the most important people in the
world. Without salespeople nothing would be sold. This
may seem obvious, but many of us hold a distorted
perception of salespeople. We consider them annoying
pests who won't leave us alone. Maybe some are, but, when
you think about it, we are all salespeople, aren't we? We all
sell ourselves in one way or another.

When we are looking to find a mate, we have to sell
ourselves or we don't get the prize. When we go for a job
interview, we have to sell ourselves or we starve. Yes, we
are all in the business of selling, and it is therefore
important that we all master the techniques that can make
us sales superstars.

One of the reasons why some people struggle through
life is that they are unable to sell themselves. This applies to
careers and to relationships; both involve the skill of
influencing others. The salesperson who procrastinates
about making calls to prospects, the man who puts off
approaching an attractive woman and asking her to go on a

---

date are both people who are struggling with a distorted self-image. These are people who hold limiting beliefs about themselves.

But remember what we learned earlier in this book. Beliefs are just beliefs. They are perceptions, and not who we *really* are. If you, for example, were to take a good look back into your past, you are likely to find an event or a series of events that have influenced your current self-image. Does your inner salesman need a shake? The good news is that it is not necessary to start analysing the past. What you can do now is to start creating a new positive self-image that will turn you into the amazing salesperson you deserve to be.

Exercise

Close your eyes and relax. Think back to a time in the past when you performed poorly in your sales environment. Maybe you were criticised about your presentation or cracked under the pressure. Or you might choose to think back to a time when you were rejected by a member of the opposite sex – an event that you feel could be influencing your behaviour now. Imagine the event up on a large movie screen in your mind.

Run the event forward, seeing, hearing and feeling the memory. Make sure you are watching yourself in the movie. When you have finished running the movie, go back to the beginning and run it again, this time adding any extra detail you may have missed the first time. Now imagine running the movie backwards, as if you are rewinding a film on the screen. Do this 10 times, as fast as you can.

Now go back to the beginning and TRY to run the movie forward at normal speed. You may find this more difficult now, and the memory likely holds less emotional charge. If you can still run the movie forward as normal, you'll need to run it back another five times.

When you find that your perception of the memory has changed, run a new movie, seeing, feeling and hearing yourself responding in the way you would have liked it to have happened.

Repeat this process on all similar events, coming right up to the present day. This process will help to erase any negative imprints that could be holding you back today.

The next step is to mentally rehearse yourself acting as you desire to become in the future. Run the movie again and again, seeing, hearing and feeling yourself acting as if you are an effective and confident salesperson. Now step into the movie and connect to the feelings. Imagine the feelings of total self-confidence surging through your body.

Step back out of the image again and visualise all the people who you trust and admire (such as your friends, family and colleagues, etc.) in the movie. See them cheering you on, praising you and complimenting you.

Continue to practise this mental rehearsal each day for 30 minutes.

You can do this in one sitting (morning or afternoon) or you might practise twice each day, in two 15-minute sessions. Make sure you add as much detail as possible each time. If you can't think of any earlier memories, just focus on the second step of the exercise – the mental-rehearsal part.

It's great to develop a positive self-image and it's also important. It is, however, equally important to be able put yourself into the necessary state, in order to perform at your very best on the day. Everybody experiences problems and everybody has 'off 'days. The problem is, of course, that we don't always know when we are going to get them. All great salespeople know how to get themselves into a winning state. I say 'winning', because salespeople have the same mindset as athletes. It's about winning the game. We could look at life as a game, and many successful people do just that. In reality, everybody wants to win; it's something that is programmed into most of us from childhood. People who look at life as a battle get just that, a battle. How do you look at life? Is it a game or a battle?

Exercise

This is a great way to get yourself into a winning state.

Put yourself into a comfortably relaxed state. Imagine yourself floating back to a time where you felt high in energy, focused and confident. As you go there, see what you saw, hear what you heard and feel what you felt.

Imagine how you looked, your posture, and the sound of your voice – in particular, the tonality. How did you feel? Notice the energy inside your body. When you find yourself back in this state, gently press your thumb and forefinger together. As you do this repeat a word or phrase to yourself that matches your experience. For example: 'Go for it', 'In the zone' or 'Ready for action'; whatever feels right to you. Now relax your fingers and come back to full awareness. Let your mind clear and gently press your thumb and finger together again. You'll start to get the positive feelings back again. If you find you don't, go back and repeat the exercise.

Whenever you need to get back into this state in the future, just relax for a few moments, squeeze your thumb and finger together, and allow yourself to go back into the wining state again. Successful salespeople work hard, and need to work hard on *themselves* – mentally, physically and emotionally. Without harmony in these key areas, the risk of burn-out or other stress-related illness is greatly increased. The need for mind/body breaks and emotional control is vital for maximum success. It is easy to neglect these areas in this crazy, fast-moving world we live in, but ignore them at your own peril.

> **SUCCESS SECRET**
> You become what you think about all day.

CHAPTER 19

How to Sleep Soundly

Health is the first muse, and sleep is the
condition to produce it.
RALPH WALDO EMERSON

There is probably nothing worse than lack of sleep. We might feel tired after a bad night's sleep, but that's nothing compared to the other problems that insomnia can lead to. Lack of concentration, low energy levels and anxiety are just some of the symptoms of insomnia, which can become entirely debilitating.

There are several ways in which insomnia can manifest itself. You may waken early and stay awake, waken several times during the night and find it impossible to drift off again, or you may simply find it impossible to *get* to sleep, no matter what time you hit the pillow. Some people experience a combination or even *all* of these symptoms.

Imagine how your life would change as a result of sleeping well? You would have more energy, you would feel happier, you would be able to concentrate better, and you would be able to control your weight more easily. Yet millions of people go through life accepting sleepless nights and broken sleep. *You can change this*. It's interesting to note that people who don't sleep well are usually highly motivated individuals. They try to get to sleep while simultaneously planning the next day. Needless to say, this doesn't work. For natural, deep sleep to occur, you need to be relaxed.

When your mind is overactive, you are literally keeping yourself awake with your loud internal dialogue. The next time you find yourself lying awake at night, tune into your internal dialogue, and become aware of the volume of your self-talk. You will probably notice that you are talking to yourself in a loud, excited way.

Imagine your internal dialogue has a volume control – visualise it in your mind. Reach out in your imagination, and start to turn the volume down. Hear your voice becoming increasingly softer, increasingly quieter. With some practice, you will find you are able to turn down your internal dialogue whenever you need to, which will help you to relax more.

So what stops us from sleeping? Every one of us has a different reason, or combination of causes; however, most of us struggle to sleep because of:

- unresolved problems
- anxiety about an upcoming event
- physical pain
- too much caffeine or other stimulants
- eating too close to bedtime
- excitement
- a bedroom that is too hot or too light, or even just cluttered
- noise.

What stops *you* from sleeping?

ACCESSING SLEEP MEMORIES

In a trance state you can access memories of sleep. San Antonio clinician Richard Garver has found that our minds store memories for almost everything we do, and that includes our sleep patterns. You can relax yourself into a trance and ask your unconscious mind to review your patterns of healthy sleep. The reality is that even when we are in the deepest sleep, we are never really completely unconscious.

Exercise

Close your eyes and allow yourself to relax deeply. Allow yourself some time to really relax and let go. Now, suggest to yourself: *I would like my subconscious mind to recall healthy sleep memories now ... and have them occur tonight as I lie comfortably in bed.*

Exercise

Is lack of sleep getting you down? Try thinking *blue*. Let's get started.

Go to bed and *try* to stay awake for 90 minutes. As you do this, close your eyes and think *blue*. Imagine all your thoughts are the colour blue. Anything you imagine should be coloured in shades of blue. *Think blue*.

It is important that you really *try* to stay awake for 90 minutes. Remember, the more you try to stay awake the more difficult it becomes. As you lie in your bed, say to yourself: *I try to stay awake for 90 minutes.* When you do this, you are using the law of reversed effort (see page 10).

USING YOUR INSOMNIA

If you are not asleep 30 minutes after going to bed, get up and do something. The important thing here is to make sure you do something that you really don't *like* to do. Maybe it's your accounts, cleaning your car or the kitchen drawer, or sorting socks. Choose something you find mind-numbingly boring. Do this until you find yourself becoming sleepy and then go back to bed. You may have to do this several times, but eventually your subconscious mind will think: *Oh no! Not the accounts again!* and send you off to sleep.

Exercise

Another great technique is to offer your subconscious mind some suggestions, and it's very easy and natural to do this when you are relaxing into trance.

As you relax, say to yourself: *As my head makes contact with the pillow, I find myself feeling more and more tired … I am aware of my eyes becoming more and more heavier, with each minute that passes … I can try to open my eyes, but I find them becoming more and more heavier … the more I try to stay awake, the more tired I feel … because I am drifting more deeply into a comfortable, easy slumber … and I don't know if I start to lose awareness of my arms before or after my legs … and I wonder whether I am going to enjoy a light rest, a medium rest or maybe a deep, deep slumber.*

Experiment with the above exercises. Another good idea is to practise one of the relaxation exercises (see pages 83 to 86). Relaxation is a crucial part of getting a good night's sleep, and if you can crack that, you are halfway there.

CHAPTER 20

OVERCOMING A FEAR OF FLYING

Only your mind can produce fear.
A COURSE IN MIRACLES

Over the years I have helped many people overcome a fear of flying. There are many phobias that can affect us, but as most hypnotherapists will agree, the fear of flying is not only the most common, but also one of the most debilitating. Why? Let's be honest; there aren't that many snakes in Britain, and the type of spiders we see in this country can normally be avoided if we run fast enough. But fear of flying? That's a different story. We humans are programmed towards pleasure, and flying has become a key element of the pursuit of pleasure in the modern-day world. It's fun to travel to exotic places, a relief to take time off work and get away to sunnier, more adventurous or more relaxing climes, and it provides a perfect breather to our busy daily lives.

The subconscious mind is a breeding ground for phobias. You may have forgotten what caused the phobia of flying (or, indeed, any other phobia), but your subconscious mind most certainly hasn't. The trigger for your fear could have been something that happened some 30 years ago. Maybe you were flying over the Atlantic Ocean and the plane got caught in some serious turbulence. After being thrown around in your seat for several minutes or more, in a state of sheer fear you affirm to yourself that you will not fly again *ever*. Zing! You have a phobia. The subconscious has not only absorbed your affirmation, but because you were in a state of terror (a state of heightened emotion), the impact was even more profound.

So, you decide you don't like flying any more; you might even justify this with your conscious mind and tell yourself that your travelling days are over – you've seen and done everything you want to do. A part of you might present the niggling feeling that you are frightened because of that scary experience, but it's more likely that your conscious mind will admit being 'put off' rather than accepting that you have acquired a full-blown phobia.

It is interesting to note that we are only born with two natural phobias – a fear of falling and a fear of loud noises. The rest are created by life events that involve feelings of fear. But the good news is that you *can* overcome your flying phobia and, in most cases, you can do it quickly.

Exercise

There are seven main steps to this exercise, and once you've achieved them, you'll need to practise them for a few weeks.

- *Step 1*. Close your eyes and relax. Imagine all your muscles becoming loose and comfortable, from the top of your head down to the tips of your toes. You can deepen your relaxation by slowly counting backwards from 100 to zero, letting the muscles in your body soften and relax with each number you count.

- *Step 2*. Imagine you are at the airport with your family or friends. Hear the sounds of the planes, see the people around you, feel the feelings of relaxation inside your body. Imagine yourself feeling calm and relaxed.
- Now, step out of the event and watch yourself walking on to the plane...
- Watch yourself through the window sitting comfortably, looking calm and relaxed, happy and confident.
- *Step 3*. Picture the plane taking off. Hear it. See it. Imagine you are like Superman or Supergirl flying along next to the plane, seeing yourself through the window looking happy, confident and relaxed. Continue the journey all the way to your destination. Seeing yourself looking happy, confident and relaxed.
- *Step 4*. Repeat the process coming home. Imagine yourself flying next to the plane, seeing yourself looking comfortable, relaxed and in control. Picture yourself walking off the plane, relaxed and confident.
- *Step 5*. Now repeat the process, this time imagining that you are travelling inside the plane feeling calm and relaxed. Feel yourself relaxing back comfortably in your seat, listening to your favourite piece of music or enjoying a good movie. Rehearse the journey all the way there and back.
- *Step 6*. Slowly bring yourself back to full awareness by slowly counting up from one to five.
- *Step 7*. Practise positive self-talk, based on the

principles of hypnotic language; for example, *I choose to feel relaxed as I fly because I love to travel.*

Practise this exercise every day for three weeks and have a great flight!

CHAPTER 21

UNLOCKING YOUR CREATIVE MIND

When we are no longer able to change a situation, we are challenged to change ourselves.
VICTOR FRANKL

The number-one trait of a genius mind is said to be creative power. Just look at all the so-called geniuses of our time, and you'll see that they all have an abundance of creativity. And, in many ways, the key message of this book is about how to use your creativity to change your life. By now you have discovered that your mind designs your life. This effectively makes you a genius, because most people do not realise the importance of using the mind as a creative force. When you master the skill of self-hypnosis you literally become a creative genius, for the simple act of relaxing your mind will start the creative process. In fact, relaxation strengthens the mind. Where most of us go wrong is trying to use our *will* to *try* to change, which normally fails. Why? Because we aren't in communication with our creative selves. Change has nothing to do with being intellectual or intelligent, for we can't use our intellect to change our behaviour; instead, we must use our creative minds to create change.

FAILURE CAN HELP MAKE YOU MORE CREATIVE

Can it be a coincidence that the most successful and most creative people have all experienced failure? It has been shown that failure can and does enhance creativity – providing, of course, that we don't give up at the first hurdle. The secret is to think of failure as being temporary, and an opportunity for personal growth. This might be the reason why most highly successful people don't get it right the first time. Perhaps failure could be the key to unlocking our inner potential.

The following advice can help you to improve both your creativity *and* your health.

WALKING: THE KEY TO CREATIVITY AND LIVING LONGER

Walking is the king of exercise. It keeps us fit and healthy, it helps prevent heart disease, and it has a relaxing effect upon our minds and bodies. Walking tends to clear the mind, and many of us use walking to think things over and get our creative juices flowing. Walking is a completely natural form of activity and most of us are able to manage to walk to some degree.

What many people are unaware of is the fact that after a period of walking, we tend to drift into an altered state of awareness. As we walk, we tend to focus inward; we experience a free-flowing of thoughts and images. When we walk in natural surroundings, we begin to tune into the beauty around us. It provides the perfect environment to listen for ideas and solutions to present problems. Experiment with 20 to 30 minutes of walking each day.

THE MAGIC OF SILENCE

Silence has power. It may well be one of the most powerful things that we can experience. In our busy, hectic lives it's very rare we take time to just sit – or as the poet William Henry Davies once said, 'stand and stare'. We rarely take time to tune into the stillness, which leads us into our minds. You may be thinking that this sounds somewhat like meditation, and you're right. We all need to learn to meditate on silence. The problem is that many of us find this difficult because we are conditioned to live in a rather noisy environment, and we fill it with even more distractions, such as radios, televisions, games consoles and phones, which create even more noise. Most of us find doing nothing, and seeking silence, quite challenging.

Imagine sitting peacefully and quietly for 20 minutes to a hour each day. As each day passes, it becomes easier, as your thoughts begin to slow down. Your body releases stress and your creativity starts to flow. And as the weeks pass, you notice that you are dealing with stress more easily. You feel calmer and happier, you begin to experience more creativity, and you seem to have more energy. This is the power of silence. Many people report they feel more spiritual and closer to their inner nature when they take the time to find and use silence.

This does not have to be a difficult process. There is no need to learn complicated mantras or visualisations. You simply need to sit back and let nature do its work. The best time to do this is first thing in the morning, when the world has not got moving yet. There are fewer distractions, and far less noise; your mind is clearer, and you normally haven't had the opportunity to focus on worries or concerns. When you wake up, you are naturally closer to your inner nature.

All you have to do is get out of your bed, perform your ablutions, and then sit comfortably somewhere for at least 20 minutes. It's best to begin with this length of time, and then build up slowly to an hour. At the outset, handing over 20 minutes of your busy morning might seem daunting, but as you begin to experience the profound benefits of this morning ritual, you'll find it easier and even pleasurable to get up a little earlier.

Exercise

Sit in a relaxed position. There is no need to do anything. Just close your eyes. As your mind begins to become still, just be aware of your existence, your breathing and thoughts, and the sensations in your body. If your mind starts to get busy with thoughts, just notice the thoughts and let them go. Don't hold on to anything.

Become an observer of yourself. Listen to your inner nature for a change.

Get to know yourself a little. You may be surprised by what you discover – how amazing you are, for example – and your creativity will soar.

UNLOCKING YOUR CREATIVITY

Research has shown the following approaches to be helpful in unlocking creativity, and these can be used whether you are temporarily struggling with creativity, or even if you feel that you've never had a creative bone in your body.

- Become fascinated with new interesting things and places.
- Take regular breaks.
- Surround yourself with interesting people.
- Become aware of early-morning thoughts.

CHAPTER 22

HOW TO TURN PROBLEMS INTO SOLUTIONS

Every problem contains the seeds of its own solution.
STANLEY ARNOLD

There is always more than one way to look at anything. For example, imagine that you want to lose weight. You might think to yourself: 'I have tried all my life to control my weight without success'. But you also feel that you have learned what works and what doesn't. You might say to yourself, 'My job is so boring', which leads you to the conclusion that you are ready for bigger challenges. This is called 'reframing'. Any time we choose to see the positive of a situation, we are putting it into a new frame.

Focusing on the negative can create a great deal of stress. When you start to become more aware of the images you are making in your mind through your words, you are in a better position to change them. So whenever you find yourself looking at the negative of a situation, *stop.* Take a few moments to find the positive side. This is a good habit to get into, because when you train yourself to focus on the bright side of things, life becomes more rewarding. You begin to discover more opportunity for yourself.

Exercise

Write down 10 negative experiences you have had in your life. Now reframe those experiences into positive experiences.

CHANGING YOUR PERSPECTIVE

One definition of a 'problem' is 'being stuck'. Unable to make difficult decisions, overeating, feeling anxious, and lacking confidence may all be symptoms of being 'stuck', and when we enter this state, we are only able to see things from our own perspective. It is difficult to find solutions when we view things from the same angle. The great psychologist Fritz Pearls, the founder of Gestalt therapy, said, 'Sometimes we need to lose our mind, and come to our senses.'

Now before you think I have gone mad, let me explain what Pearls meant: anything that breaks the pattern that is creating the problem can be helpful to the process of becoming unstuck.

Exercise

This will help you to change your perspective on a problem.

Stand in the middle of a large room. As you stand there, become aware of the way you feel about the problem. Put yourself right smack in the middle of the feeling that is attached to the problem. Make sure you get a good representation of what it is you want to feel different about. This is your own point of view.

Now move to a corner of the room and imagine you are taking the position of other people who are involved in helping you change, or who are supporting you. This might be your family, friends, coach or therapist. Take their perspective, as you look over at yourself in the middle of the room – back at position number one. Imagine what they would say about your situation. Now move to a third position, and take the role of a complete outsider, somebody who is uninvolved. Take their perspective on things.

After spending some time on this, move back to the first position and check how you feel. You will be surprised how different you feel about things now.

HOW TO LAUGH AT YOUR PROBLEMS

Ever found yourself thinking: 'One day I will look back and laugh at this.' What's stopping you from laughing now? I can tell you the main reason: you are looking at the problem as a problem. If you continue to look at something in the same way, you will continue to feel the same feelings. Maybe you can't just change the problem that quickly – for whatever reason – but you *can* change the way you picture it.

When you continue to focus on something in the same way, you inject more and more energy into the problem. We all have the ability to change our perspective on things, and we can all see things differently. So why not use your mind allow yourself to laugh at your problems. Humour is one of the most powerful healers. In his wonderful book, *Anatomy of an Illness as Perceived by the Patient*, Norman Cousins talks about how humour helped him to overcome a painful condition. Cousins sat and watched his favourite comedy movies for hours. The release of pain-killing endorphins from his brain had a numbing effect on his discomfort.

Exercise

This exercise will help you to inject a little humour into any situation or problem.

Close your eyes and imagine a situation or person that is causing you some anxiety or distress. Notice whether you see yourself in the image or whether you are looking out of your own eyes. If the event or image is unpleasant for you, you are probably looking out of your own eyes, as if you are there (although not always). Become aware of any sounds. Become aware of how you feel. Notice whether there are any sounds around you. Is the image in colour or black and white? Sense the whole event around you. Become aware of what you are experiencing emotionally.

Now make a few changes. If the image is in colour, drain the colour out. If you are looking out of your own eyes, imagine stepping out of the image and looking at yourself in the situation. Are there any sounds? If there are, turn the volume down. If the image is large, make it smaller. If what you are experiencing is the opposite of what I have suggested, *then do the opposite* – for example, step into the image, turn up the colour, or make it bigger and brighter.

Now, imagine the whole event in cartoon form. Add some funny music or some circus music. Give people funny faces and big feet. If you are seeing the event as a movie, run it backwards quickly or very slowly. Maybe you are viewing the event as a still picture; if you are, turn it into a movie, and give it some movement.

How do you feel about the event now? My guess is that it seems different. How can this be? You have used your mind to view things in a different way, a way that you now feel more comfortable about. Think about how you can use this technique with other negative situations in your life.

Exercise

This will help you to reframe the problem – literally!

Close your eyes and go inside. Make an image of the situation or concern you have. Explore the image. Is it in colour, or black and white? Is it a still frame or maybe you see it as a movie? Notice if there is any sound. Become aware of the feelings that go with it. Now imagine putting it in a large frame. Visualise it with a thick golden frame around it. As you do this, shrink the image and move it further away. Notice how you feel differently about the situation now.

THINK, TO PLAY THE GAME OF LIFE

If you think about it, life is pretty much a sport – isn't it? We are all playing the 'game of life'. Some people may not like to think of it like this, but it's close to the truth. We are trying to play the game of having more money, having a better home or a better car, or maybe finding a better partner. We are constantly trying to compete with ourselves and others. We follow the rules of the game, which can also trap us into playing more competitively, whether we like it or not.

We are all goal-driven to a degree – some more than others. Without goals life would be fairly meaningless, as we'd be treading water rather than moving towards the other side. I don't mean everyone has *big* goals; instead, there are goals such as getting a job, paying the rent on time, and even just surviving.

And in the game of life, just as in any sporting game, we are all trying to achieve something. That's one reason why many of the mind-programming techniques that are so successfully used in sport can be used in general life as well.

Most of us want to 'win' the game of life, and there is nothing wrong with this. A lot of it has to do with our programming. When an athlete gets ready for competition, he has to prepare himself mentally as well as physically. He begins to think in a certain way, he eats in a different way, he rests more, and he finds himself becoming more aware. He is more focused and more in tune with his winning mindset.

An athlete's preparation is not too far away from what has to happen for someone who is highly motivated to achieve something worthwhile. Imagine if we could develop an athlete's mindset ourselves, as a tool for reaching our own life desires. It doesn't matter whether it's to make more money, to be healthier, to stop smoking, or even to become a kinder, more spiritual human being. You can programme your mind to win in the game of life.

THE SUCCESS HOUR

Imagine becoming a national expert in almost anything you desire, in just three years! Impossible you might think? No, not impossible, challenging. The truth is that most people don't achieve this, or anything like it, but I can tell you now that *anyone* can achieve this with desire and the right attitude, and it can be undertaken in the comfort of your own home. Here's what you need to do.

First you have to know what you want to become an expert in. This for many is perhaps the biggest challenge.

What do you want to do with your life? Write a book, or maybe develop a whole new career? For some subjects you may need to go to college or attend training to get the basic grounding, but once you have got that, you can then use a powerful formula to become a true expert.

To become an expert in almost anything, study your chosen subject for *one hour* each day for three years. Added on to any basic training that might be required, this will guarantee that you achieve expert status. It has been said that you can become a national expert in three years and an international expert in five! Imagine that!

So what does that have to do with making changes in your life? Well, apart from the obvious benefits of personal self-improvement, doing this can be a life-changing experience. You can develop money-making skills that may lead to financial freedom. You could develop the framework for a whole new career. You could use your new skills and knowledge to help others. You could expand your creativity and brain power to such an extent that new doors open all over the place. The opportunities are infinite, and the only limitation lies in your own imagination.

We have all heard of at least one person who has taken a major new turning in their lives. And most of us have thought to ourselves, 'Well, if he can do it, so can I!' So why don't you? What do you want to do with your life? Are you the type of person who doesn't like to take risks or hates change? If you are, join the club, because no-one really does.

Success and behaviour psychology guru Dr Robert Anthony said. 'We fear the thing we want the most.' He couldn't be more right. It's just too easy to stay in our own comfort zone, but is that how life is supposed to be? I don't think so, nor do you, deep down. Let's face it many things we do in life involve some risk; we have to take some chances. It is reported that the biggest regret that many people have as they near the ends of the lives is that they didn't 'go for it' more. They didn't grab the chances offered to them, and move outside the comfort of their individual box.

As we get older many of us develop a sense of urgency about life. All of a sudden we become aware that time is moving fast. Maybe this is nature's way of telling us to get off our backsides, and to start living. A great way to start is to find out what you want, commit to it for an hour every day, and then go for it.

THE POWER OF MAN

According to legend, many years ago, high up on Mount Olympus, the gods created man. They wanted to make man in the same image of themselves – powerful. The challenge was, where would they put man's power where he would not easily find it? You see, the gods were worried because if man was to find his power to easily, he might use it to overthrow them and they wouldn't want that to happen.

Night after night, the gods sat around the campfire high up in the mountains discussing where to hide man's power.

One god said, 'Let's put it deep in the heart of the forest; he will never get to it there.'

Another god said, 'I know, let's put at the bottom of the ocean.'

But the gods all disagreed. No, if he's as clever as we are, he'll find it in all of those places. And so they continued, night after night, discussing where to put man's power.

'Let's put it deep inside a cave, with a large boulder over the opening, to prevent him from getting in,' said a god.

'No, let's put it high up on a mountain,' said another.

But all the gods agreed that man would be just too smart, and he'd soon find that power and find a way to use it.

And so they continued, night after night, discussing where they could put man's power.

After much deliberation, and many long nights, one god

stood up and said excitedly, 'I have it! I know where we can put man's power, where he'll *never* think to look'.

The gods looked at him with anticipation.

The god smiled, and said, 'Right inside himself. He will never think to look there.'

Have you?

For more information, personal hypnotherapy sessions, or support, visit www.marcus-dsilva.com or email me at info@marcus-dsilva.com.